FLOWERING CHERRY

A Play in Two Acts

by

ROBERT BOLT

SAMUEL

GW00634137

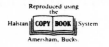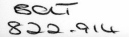

FLOWERING CHERRY

Produced at the Theatre Royal, Haymarket, London, on the 21st November 1957, with the following cast of characters—

(in the order of their appearance)

ISOBEL CHERRY	*Celia Johnson*
TOM CHERRY, her son	*Andrew Ray*
JIM CHERRY, her husband	*Ralph Richardson*
GILBERT GRASS	*Frederick Piper*
JUDY CHERRY, the daughter	*Dudy Nimmo*
DAVID BOWMAN	*Brewster Mason*
CAROL, an Art Student	*Susan Burnet*

Directed by FRITH BANBURY
Settings designed by REECE PEMBERTON

SYNOPSIS OF SCENES

The action of the play passes in the kitchen and garden of the Cherrys' house in the suburbs of London

ACT I

An afternoon in early Spring

ACT II

One month later. Afternoon

The CURTAIN is lowered for a few moments during Act II to indicate the passage of one hour

Time—the present

FLOWERING CHERRY

ACT I

SCENE—*The kitchen and garden of the Cherrys' house in the suburbs of London. An afternoon in early Spring.*

It is a composite setting with the kitchen R and part of the back garden L. Part of the back wall of the kitchen is cut away to reveal a gauze, cyclorama backcloth, which, when illuminated, depicts a cherry orchard in full flower. A door R of the kitchen leads to the hall, front door and other parts of the house. A door L of the kitchen gives access to the garden. Below the garden door, the wall, where a fireplace is presumed to be, is cut away. In the garden part of the garden wall is seen at the back and a fence and gate L lead to the side entrance. A dustbin stands above the back door and below the fence L, the end of a flower bed, with tulips in flower, is seen. In the kitchen there is a gas stove R. Below the stove stands a table on which there is a barrel of cider. The sink is C of the back wall with a boiler R of it. Pipes from the boiler lead to a service tank off R and thence back to the sink. There is a dresser LC of the back wall. Down L, in front of the "fireplace" is a club fender. A table stands C with four chairs to it; there is an easy chair LC and another upright chair stands between the gas stove and the cider table. There is a saucepan rack in the corner up R.

When the CURTAIN rises, the stage is in darkness. The lights come up for the Orchard Vision and the music of the "Flowering Cherry" theme is heard. After half a minute the vision and music fade and the general lights come up. It is about six p.m. ISOBEL CHERRY is standing at the sink, drying cups and saucers. She is a slender woman of about forty to forty-five. She is graceful and lively but the fundamental pattern of her features is one of melancholy. The liveliness is purchased with a certain amount of strain; it is applied, though now habitual. Her dress is neat and becoming. She wears slippers and a clean, bright apron. TOM CHERRY, her son, is seated in the easy chair LC, reading. He is approaching nineteen or twenty, lean, sensitive, much occupied with styles of behaviour, but warm, and young enough to show it. After a few moments, the rattle of the letterbox off R is heard, followed by the double knock of the postman. ISOBEL raises her head.

ISOBEL. Tom. Tom.

TOM. M-hm?

ISOBEL. I think that's the post.

(TOM *does not respond.*

ISOBEL *wipes her hands, crosses and exits R*)

I

TOM (*rising and timing it so as to be just too late*) I'll get it. (*He resumes his seat without taking his attention from the book*)

(ISOBEL *enters* R. *She carries some letters and magazines*)

ISOBEL. *Farmers Weekly—Smallholder.* Mm. (*She glances at the letters, selects one, puts the others with the magazines on the table, then takes the selected letter to Tom*)

(TOM *does not notice*)

(*Irritated*) Tom!

TOM (*looking up*) Oh, Lord! (*He takes the letter and opens it*)

(ISOBEL *returns to the sink*)

ISOBEL (*tensely*) Well, tell me, you ass.

TOM. Same again. Deferred.

ISOBEL (*relaxing*) Oh.

TOM. Is that a relief?

ISOBEL (*resuming her washing-up*) You've got to go some time; the sooner the better, I suppose.

TOM (*with playful indignation*) Is that so?

ISOBEL. Certainly. Don't be so conceited.

TOM. I bet you make a scene when I do go.

ISOBEL. My goodness, you *are* conceited. I'll be glad to see the back of you.

(TOM *grunts, returns to his book, but cannot, and looks up*)

TOM. Why?

ISOBEL. To bring you to your present state of perfection, Thomas Cherry, has taken nineteen years of my life.

TOM. So?

ISOBEL. So I'll be glad to see the back of you.

TOM. Hey! Is that the truth?

ISOBEL (*conceding; with a smile*) It's not the whole truth.

TOM (*fishing*) What's the rest of it like?

ISOBEL. Complicated, sonny. Very, very complicated.

TOM (*indifferently*) Yeah. (*He nods*) Yeah. (*He returns to his book*)

ISOBEL (*turning and leaning on the sink*) Tom?

TOM. Yes?

ISOBEL. I wonder where they'll send you.

TOM. Aldershot.

ISOBEL. That'd be nice, you could get home for weekends.

TOM. I might not want to.

ISOBEL (*turning to the sink; dryly*) You would.

TOM (*surprised*) Wouldn't you want me to?

ISOBEL. We'll keep a light burning in the window.

TOM (*angrily*) What's the matter with you, anyway?

ISOBEL. Nothing. I'm talking over your head, that's all. I can still talk over your head, you know.

TOM. Well, I'm glad it gives you so much pleasure. (*He returns to his book*) You've been alive twice as long—(*sulkily*) it'd be a poor look-out if you couldn't.

(ISOBEL *turns her head, smiles at* TOM's *sulking back, then moves down* C)

ISOBEL. Look, Tom, when the post comes, and I'm washing up, don't say "I'll get it", and sit there reading T. S. Eliot. Either stay where you are and tell me to get it, or say "I'll get it"—and get it.

TOM. Sorry. You're making a lot of it, aren't you?

(ISOBEL *sits on the chair* L *of the table and looks over the back of it at* TOM)

ISOBEL. No, Tom, it's an attitude. Either do things or don't do them, but whichever it is, know it. Otherwise, as sure as fate, you'll end up like . . . (*She breaks off*) It's a terrible habit that "I'll get it" and sitting where you are. It's shifty.

TOM. Yes. Like "D'you want a drink, old chap?" when you want one yourself.

ISOBEL (*coldly*) We're talking about you, now, nobody else; and it's shifty. (*Urgent and appealing*) I'm a little bit worried about you, Tom, because you're going away soon and you know we have had this trouble in the past about not speaking the truth, and not being quite careful about money—and you're going away and I don't want you to—I don't want you to be . . .

TOM (*rejecting her warmth with injured pride*) Shifty.

ISOBEL. Yes.

TOM (*coldly*) Well, don't worry; I dare say I'll end up in the dog-house—(*he shakes his head rhythmically*) but not like the Old Man.

ISOBEL (*rising and moving to the sink; defeated*) I've asked you not to call him that. (*She prepares a cauliflower for cooking*)

(TOM *resumes reading*)

CHERRY (*off* L) Come in and have a drink, Gilbert.

(CHERRY *enters in the garden* L.

GILBERT GRASS *follows him on.* CHERRY *is a burly man of about fifty with a round red face and thinning grey hair. His carriage is confident, his expression heavy, but there is about the eyes and mouth the sadness and confusion of the immature. His clothes are good and timidly sportif, of earth colours, and include a trilby turned down back and front and a fawn waistcoat with leather buttons.* GRASS *is more correctly dressed in a city suit, but in the subtle gradations of cut and buttoning his clothes express that he is a junior figure to Cherry. He is an undersized, bespectacled man with a face boldly designed to express fear, but wearing the covert confidence of those not hampered by self-respect. Either he was formed by Nature for office life or office life has formed his nature; either way he is a condemnation of it.* CHERRY *holds the gate open.* GRASS *crosses below Cherry to* R *of him.* CHERRY *then closes the gate and stands down* L)

GRASS. Oh, well—mm—ha-ha . . .

CHERRY. This way. Tiptoe through the tulips.

GRASS. Very pretty.

CHERRY. Dutch bulbs.

GRASS. Are they? Pretty. (*Eagerly*) Go on.

CHERRY. Oh, well, then I said: "If people don't want to buy insurance, good luck to them. I'm not insured myself."

GRASS (*admiringly*) Are you not?

CHERRY (*sturdily*) No, that's not the way to live. Look at it this way: You can't insure happiness, can you? You can't ensure that you'll get on with your wife—for example. You take it from me, Gilbert, if a thing can be insured—it's not worth insuring.

GRASS. Oh, dear.

CHERRY. It isn't.

GRASS. I shall have to think about that.

CHERRY (*knocking out his pipe on his shoe*) Well, that's what I told him.

GRASS (*prompting*) Yes?

CHERRY. "That's not the way to live," I said. "I *despise* people who buy insurance."

GRASS. Good Heavens! What did he say?

CHERRY. Och, you know what he's like.

GRASS. He wasn't rude, I hope.

CHERRY. Rude? No, he wasn't rude. "That's a very peculiar attitude for our sales manager to have," he said. (*He crosses below Grass to* R *of him*)

GRASS. Oh, dear.

CHERRY. I wasn't going to let him get away with that——

GRASS. No.

CHERRY. —so I said, quietly—I didn't want a row—"are you dissatisfied with my work? Because if you are," I said—(*here he forgets that he is recounting a tale and begins to lose and listen to himself*) "you can give the job to someone else; I don't want it. As a matter of fact," I said, "this entire establishment makes me vomit. And you can keep the job." (*He moves on to the kitchen doorstep*)

GRASS. Gracious Heavens, do you mean you've given notice?

CHERRY. What does it sound like?

GRASS. But . . .

CHERRY (*turning at the door*) Er—keep it under your hat, old man.

GRASS. Oh, yes, yes. But . . .

(CHERRY *comes into the kitchen, crosses to Isobel, kisses her, then stands above the table.* GRASS *follows Cherry into the kitchen, closes the door and stands just inside it.* Tom *rises, then sits on the upstage seat of the fender*)

Cherry. Hello, darling.

Isobel. Hello, darling.

Grass. Good evening, Mrs Cherry; I'm here again.

Isobel. How are you, Mr Grass?

Grass. Nicely, thank you.

Cherry (*picking up the magazines from the table; with satisfaction*) Ah! (*He unwraps the magazines and inspects them almost feverishly*)

Isobel. Had a good day?

Cherry. About usual.

Grass. Oh, hardly that, I think.

Isobel. Oh?

Cherry (*putting down the magazines*) Have a chair, Gilbert. (*He goes to the dresser and collects a pint mug and a glass*) I'll draw you a drink. (*He crosses to the barrel* R *and draws a glass of cider for Grass*)

Grass (*moving down* C; *with a curious cringing eagerness for trouble*) No, indeed, a momentous day, I should have said.

Cherry (*to Isobel*) Glass for you, darling?

Isobel. Not now, darling. (*To Grass*) What happened?

Grass (*ducking his head fussily*) No, no, no, it's your husband's news, not mine.

Isobel (*moving to* R *of the table and looking from Cherry to Grass*) What news?

Grass. No, no, no, he should bear his own good tidings. (*He sits in the chair* L *of the table*) I feel they are good tidings; I know Mr Cherry does. (*He is a little breathless at his own temerity, but helpless*)

Isobel. Well, Jim?

Cherry (*crossing and handing the glass of cider to Grass*) You're being a bit tactless, old man. (*He returns to the barrel and fills the mug for himself*)

Grass (*promptly abasing himself*) I do beg your pardon. I'll say no more. (*He hides behind his glass, from which he takes tiny sips*)

Cherry. Damage is done now.

(Tom *sits very still, but is very attentive*)

Isobel. Do tell me. What happened, Mr Grass?

Grass. I really don't think I ought . . .

Tom (*rising*) Come on, Mr Grass, you've got nicely started.

Cherry (*moving up* C; *furiously*) Oh, you're there, are you? (*He pauses*) I've given notice, that's all.

Tom. Given notice?

Cherry. Do you mind?

Tom. On the contrary. (*He resumes his seat*)

Cherry (*happy to hide fear of his wife behind rage with his son*) That's a relief. I shouldn't like to do anything *you* disapproved of.

(TOM *returns to his book*)

ISOBEL. How did it happen?

CHERRY (*at Tom*) It would upset me dreadfully to think I had lost *your* good opinion.

ISOBEL. When? Today? This afternoon?

CHERRY (*at Tom*) That has been my principal preoccupation, of course. My first thought naturally was to wonder if *you* would approve of it.

ISOBEL (*with sudden anger*) Jim!

CHERRY (*facing Isobel with the aid of his temper*) Well?

ISOBEL. Have you?

CHERRY. I've just said so, haven't I?

ISOBEL. But definitely?

GRASS (*with an admiring chuckle*) More than definitely, emphatically.

ISOBEL. But, Jim . . .

CHERRY. What's the matter?

ISOBEL. Let me get used to it. You've actually done it.

CHERRY. Why not, dammit?

ISOBEL (*passing her hand over her head and laughing*) I dunno. There must be some reason why people don't. (*She moves to the gas stove*)

(CHERRY *drains his mug*)

CHERRY. Cowardice! That's what stops 'em. Gilbert'd give notice if he dared. (*He crosses to the barrel*)

GRASS. Oh . . .

CHERRY (*turning with relief to Grass*) Yes, you would. You tell yourself you wouldn't, but you would. That's what this lousy life does for a man. It rots you. It's artificial.

GRASS (*to Isobel*) There's a lot in it, you know.

CHERRY (*refilling his mug*) Don't tell me, old man, I know. If you'd ever known a natural life—a life close to the earth, you'd understand all right. (*He moves above the table, puts down his mug and picks up a magazine*) Well, that's what I came from, and that's what I'm going back to.

GRASS. Ah, those orchards of yours.

(*The music of the "Flowering Cherry" theme is heard.* CHERRY, *during the first part of his following speech, unwraps the magazine and scatters the wrapping paper*)

CHERRY. That's it. Apples, fifteen acres, bush trees—no picking difficulties; thorough pest control and—*proper grading;* there's a fortune in it. And allow me to tell you that fifteen acres of apple trees in blossom, with a few white hens on the grass, perhaps, and some high white clouds in a blue sky, like you get it in May and early June down there; it's a sight for the gods, it's Shangri-la.

GRASS (*raising his glass; solemnly*) And here's to your success.
CHERRY (*picking up his mug*) I appreciate that, Gilbert.

(GRASS *and* CHERRY *drink.* ISOBEL *moves to* R *of the table*)

(*He sits on the chair above the table*) Of course, it's going to be damned hard work. Nobody knows that better than me.

(*The music fades*)

ISOBEL. How did it happen, Jim?
CHERRY (*vaguely*) Oh, I had a bit of a row . . .
ISOBEL. Who with?
CHERRY (*waving his mug; unwillingly*) Ooh . . .
GRASS. Mr Burridge, wasn't it?
ISOBEL. You had a row with Mr Burridge?
CHERRY (*roaring*) D'you think I'm afraid of him?
ISOBEL. Well, no.
CHERRY. Afraid of Burridge!
ISOBEL. He *is* your boss.
CHERRY. Not any more he isn't. (*He laughs*)
ISOBEL (*brightly*) Well, that's that, then. (*She turns and moves to the door* R)
CHERRY (*rising and following Isobel; immediately anxious*) Where are you going, 'Bel?
ISOBEL. Oh, I've got things to do.
CHERRY (*uneasily*) Well, what about it, 'Bel?
ISOBEL. Fine. I'm all for it. Excuse me, will you, Mr Grass?
CHERRY. Aren't you going to stay? Where are you going?
ISOBEL (*with sudden strain*) Oh, Jim, I've got things to do.

(ISOBEL *exits* R. TOM *watches her go*)

CHERRY. She can't take it in.
GRASS. It's natural. (*With conscious discretion*) Would you like me to go?
CHERRY (*hastily*) No. She's better left to herself.

(TOM *looks at Cherry*)

It's bound to be a shock at first, a thing like that. Women don't like change.

(TOM *turns determinedly to his book*)

(*He drains his mug, then moves up* R) Drink up, old man.
GRASS. I'm afraid I've no capacity for this stuff.
CHERRY (*bluff*) What—scrumpy?
GRASS. I like a glass of ordinary cider.
CHERRY. This *is* ordinary cider.
GRASS (*shuddering genteelly*) I don't know how you can.
CHERRY. Mind you, I'm not a serious scrumpy drinker. (*He sits on the chair* R *of the table*) Scrumpy, that's what we call it. Some

of the labourers, you know, they'll drink a couple of gallons a day as a matter of course.

GRASS. Good Heavens! It's a wonder it doesn't kill them.

CHERRY. That's a lot of rot. There was a chap on my father's farm, you never saw him without his jar of scrumpy, he slept with it on the washstand.

(*The music of the "Flowering Cherry" theme is heard*)

He lived in a little cottage—oh, five hundred years old, maybe—dark as a cave, with a big clock ticking, and as I say, this jar of scrumpy by the bed. I used to be sent down in the morning to wake him up. Well, that man was fit like an animal, beautiful, an absolute Apollo, could have lifted a horse on his back. And that was really rough scrumpy my father made. It's all made on the farms, you know.

(*The music fades*)

GRASS. Yes, I remember you telling me. It's very interesting.

CHERRY (*mechanically*) Drink up, old man. She can't get used to the idea of my not having a settled income—it's frightening to a woman.

GRASS. Oh, yes. You must give her time.

(TOM *rises, moves to the easy chair, sits and covers his ears*)

CHERRY (*rising*) Bit of luck for you, eh? (*He moves to the barrel and refills his mug*)

GRASS. Oh, I hadn't thought of it in that light.

CHERRY. I'll believe you. Thousands wouldn't. You'll get it, all right.

(GRASS *laughs*)

Senior agent, aren't you?

GRASS. Yes. Twenty-seven years on the road this November.

CHERRY. Well, then.

GRASS. Well, I won't deny I should like to come inside the office, now. In a senior capacity, of course.

CHERRY. That's only natural.

GRASS. I may say I shall have my work cut out to fill the post as well as the—er—previous incumbent.

CHERRY. You'll fill it a darn sight better, I've no illusions about that. (*He moves down* R) If I hadn't turned it in, they'd have turned me out pretty shortly.

GRASS. Oh, come now, Mr Cherry.

CHERRY (*moving up* R) By God, it's true. Old Burridge hates my guts. D'you never see him looking at me when I come in? Oh, the writing was on the wall. (*He removes his coat, puts it on the chair above the table, then stands up* L) But I can't, I can't give myself to a job like that. Those green lampshades every morning and that blasted rubber carpet. D'you know what it makes me think of?

GRASS (*ready to take the joke*) No?

CHERRY (*moving up* R) It's like walking on corpses.

GRASS. Oh, ho—that's a hot one. I know. You hate it.

CHERRY. 'Tisn't hate, exactly; it's like doom.

GRASS. Well . . .

CHERRY. "You keep the job," I said. (*He stands near the barrel.* *Brightly*) Drink up, now; there's beef in that. This chap, I'm telling you about, he always put a piece of beef in the barrel; what was his name now?

TOM (*without looking up; dryly*) Jesse Bishop.

CHERRY (*looking stonily at Tom*) That's right.

GRASS (*rising and moving up* C) Well, I must be going.

CHERRY (*moving up* R) No. Don't pay any attention to him.

GRASS. I only intended to pop in for a minute.

CHERRY (*indicating the pokers on the wall up* R) See that poker—the thick one?

GRASS. Er—yes?

CHERRY. I've seen Jesse Bishop bend a bar of iron thicker than that into a complete circle. I can bend the other one myself. (*He takes the thinner poker from the hook*) Here.

GRASS (*gingerly fingering the poker*) It's a stout piece of metal.

CHERRY. It's iron. D'you believe me? (*He holds the poker at either end and bends it into a loop*)

GRASS. Good Heavens!

(TOM *claps as though at a show*)

CHERRY (*offering the looped poker to Tom*) All right. You straighten it.

TOM. No, thanks.

CHERRY. Why not?

TOM (*attempting disdain*) It's dirty.

(CHERRY *excitedly produces a snowy white handkerchief and* *vigorously wipes the poker*)

CHERRY (*crossing to Tom*) Now it isn't. Go on, straighten it. (*He throws the handkerchief on to the table*)

TOM. No.

CHERRY. Go on.

TOM. I can't.

CHERRY. Then keep quiet. (*He throws the poker on to the table,* *picks up his mug, crosses and stands up* R)

(TOM *attempts superior eloquence, achieves sixth-form verbosity, and* *stumbles, fatally*)

TOM. I didn't know the ability to bend pokers constituted a sestival pepquit—a—an essential prerequisite of . . .

CHERRY. Aha! (*He points a finger at Tom*) You want to stick to words of one syllable. (*He turns, still malignant, moves down* R *and takes a framed reproduction from the wall over the barrel*) How d'you like this, Mr Grass?

GRASS. Gracious me, what is it?

CHERRY. Oh. This is Art.

TOM. Put it back.

CHERRY (*crossing to Grass and handing him the picture*) There you are, Mr Grass, a work of genius.

(TOM *rises*)

Someone paid five figures for the original of that.

GRASS (*tutting*) T-t-t-t.

CHERRY. Guess what that is.

GRASS (*giggling*) Could be anything.

CHERRY. That's her head. Unless it's her bottom. Very handy, you see; it's just as good either way up. (*He takes the picture from Grass and replaces it on the wall*)

GRASS. Dear, dear, dear—well, it's certainly over *my* head.

TOM. It'd be surprising if it wasn't.

CHERRY. Here! That's enough. Mr Grass is a guest in this house. They might have taught you a few manners along with your—(*contemptuously*) higher mathematics. My word, boy, you've got a rude awakening coming; they'll teach you quick enough in the army. I only hope you get an R.S.M. like one or two I've known. There's no State Scholarships there.

TOM. All right. Now, for Christ's sake, leave me alone.

CHERRY. Don't you use that language here.

TOM (*choking*) Dad, you—you make me ill. (*He throws the book on to the easy chair*) You make me sick in the guts. (*He crosses to the door* R)

CHERRY (*moving to Tom*) Thomas! (*He seizes Tom by the arm*)

(TOM *turns his face away*. CHERRY's *anger deserts him. He peers at* TOM's *face, still further averted*)

'Ey, lad. You'll grow to it. You've got a fine pair of shoulders there. You'll bend the big one some day—which is more than I can do. It's only a knack.

TOM. Let go of me.

(CHERRY *releases Tom*.
   TOM *exits* R)

CHERRY (*subdued*) He's too sensitive.

GRASS. He's very like his mother, isn't he?

CHERRY (*robustly*) Aye, that's where he gets it. Nothing sensitive about me, thank God.

GRASS (*collecting his hat and preparing to go*) Well . . .

CHERRY. Now, sit down, Gilbert. (*He crosses to the cupboard under the sink and opens it*) There's some beer in here. That's more in your line.

GRASS. No, I really must get along.

CHERRY (*holding up two bottles*) Empty. (*He puts the bottles on the table*) All right, go on, then. (*He sits on the chair above the table and opens a circular*)

GRASS. You see, my wife . . .

CHERRY. I know. She's expecting you.

GRASS (*moving to L of Cherry*) Well, the best of luck to you, Mr Cherry. I imagine we'll be seeing you at the office till the end of the month?

CHERRY. Yes. I expect they'll want me to stay on to the new quarter.

GRASS. I shouldn't let them make a convenience of you.

CHERRY. Don't worry. I'll be gone by the end of the month.

(GRASS *crosses to the door* L *and opens it.*
    ISOBEL *enters* R)

ISOBEL. Are you going, Mr Grass?

GRASS (*stopping and turning*) Well . . .

(CHERRY *rises, collects his hat, crosses to the door* L *and pushes* GRASS *in front of him*)

CHERRY. Yes, we're just going to celebrate a bit.

ISOBEL. You haven't eaten.

CHERRY. I'll be back in a jiffy. Just a couple of shorts. Come on, Gilbert.

GRASS. Oh, well . . .

CHERRY (*hustling him*) Back in a jiffy, darling.

GRASS (*peevishly*) Well, don't push me, Mr Cherry.

(GRASS *and* CHERRY *go into the garden.* ISOBEL *sits on the chair below the table, motionless, and looks at the door through which they have gone*)

CHERRY. My God, you've got big feet. "Don't push me."

GRASS (*opening the gate*) You did push me.

CHERRY. I didn't push you.

GRASS. Yes, you did.

(CHERRY *pushes* GRASS *through the gate*)

(*Peevishly*) You're still pushing me.

CHERRY. All right. I'm sorry. You coming?

GRASS. No. I must get home. I'd like to.

CHERRY. Don't apologize. I expect some of the boys will be there.

(GRASS *and* CHERRY *exit* L.
    JUDY CHERRY *enters* R. *She is about the same age as Tom, but has a manner which will be hers, barring accidents, until she is middle-aged, after which the deluge. Her glance is cold, her lips already pursed. Hygiene is her ideal, irritation her emotion, competence her*

*haven, and it is no good, of course; the something frantic behind it all is
visible. Her appearance aims at smartness, fly-away spectacles, crisp
white blouse, sensible shoes, box shouldered top coat, real hide handbag,
neat red mouth, and accentuates the angularity of her movements and
indeed of all the awkward tender surfaces she presents to life. She moves
to R of the table, puts her bag on it, then regards Isobel's back)*

JUDY. What a terrible mess! What's the matter?
ISOBEL *(without looking round, but pleasantly)* Hello, dear.
JUDY *(removing her coat and still regarding Isobel)* Where's father?
(She hangs her coat on the hooks outside the door R)
ISOBEL. He's just gone out, Judy. Do you want him?
JUDY *(moving to R of the table)* No. *(She surveys with complacent
hatred the mess Cherry has made, the magazines and wrappings strewn
about, the cider glasses, the chairs misplaced, the poker, the once white
handkerchief. She pours the cider remnants into the sink, curling her mouth
contemptuously, and leaves the glasses there)* Phew! *(She briskly collects
the waste paper and drops it into the slop can, picks up Cherry's coat and
hangs it up, then picks up the handkerchief)* This will have to be
washed.
ISOBEL. I'll take it, dear, *(She takes the handkerchief from Judy)*

*(JUDY picks up the looped poker, pulls viciously at it, then, with an
impatient exclamation, replaces it on the table. She is about to replace
the beer bottles beneath the sink, and changes her mind)*

JUDY *(meanly)* I think these can go in the dustbin. *(She crosses
to the door L)*
ISOBEL. There's some money back on those.

*(JUDY takes no notice, but goes out to the garden, throws the bottles
into the dustbin, returns to the kitchen, and closes the door)*

(Gently reproving) Judy . . .
JUDY. Well?
ISOBEL *(mildly)* Don't speak to me like that, dear. I thought
you were bringing Carol home today?
JUDY. She's coming on the bus. *(She sets the chair L of the table,
tidily under it)* She didn't come in to the studio.
ISOBEL. She doesn't seem to take her work very seriously, Judy.
JUDY *(with a private, indulgent smile)* Oh, Carol . . .
ISOBEL. I wish you'd tell us something about her.
JUDY *(defending Carol with a previously formulated conclusion; stilted)*
Actually, she's a very worthwhile person. *(She tidies the magazines)*
She's extremely attractive—one of the most popular girls at col-
lege, actually. *(She puts the chair above the table, tidily under it)* But
she has a deep inner morality that most people don't see. It's
unusual. Good-looking girls are usually so shallow.
ISOBEL. Mmm.
JUDY. I think we *shall* be able to have the flat, Mother.

Isobel. Oh?

Judy. Well, I've got the prize . . .

Isobel (*interrupting*) Yes, I know, darling. Fifty pounds is a lot of pocket money, dear, but it's *nothing* as rent.

Judy. There's something else. I—(*she makes her voice quite flat*) they're going to give me the Student Award for this year. (*She crosses above the table to* R *of it, takes cigarettes and matches from her handbag, and lights a cigarette*)

Isobel. No! Darling, when?

Judy. Mr Herring told me this morning. The Industrial Design Prof. And they'll pay me. So I'll be able to afford the flat.

Isobel. Oh. Well, it's splendid, anyway. D'you know how much?

Judy. Well, it depends. The Studentship's worth seventy-five pounds.

Isobel. Oh, very good.

Judy. And if the manufacturers take up my designs . . .

Isobel. Yes?

Judy. Well, they pay commission on the sales.

Isobel. D'you mean they'll pay you . . .?

Judy. A percentage, yes.

Isobel (*rising*) But that's wonderful! (*She pushes her chair under the table and moves to Judy*) Judy, why—(*she kisses Judy*) that's very good; a commission's rather different.

Judy (*crossing to the fender*) Now, Mother, please don't get excited.

Isobel (*following Judy*) Why not?

Judy. It doesn't *mean* anything.

Isobel. Oh, yes, it does.

Judy. It may not *lead* anywhere.

Isobel (*warmly*) Oh, you don't know. This may be very important. Things develop.

Judy. Well, I hope so, certainly, but . . .

Isobel (*laughing; protesting*) But, Judy . . .

Judy. Mother! If there's going to be a lot of—*family fuss*— I shall wish I hadn't told you.

Isobel (*still laughing*) Oh, Judy. (*Her laughter dies*) Judy, you worry me.

(Tom *enters* R)

Tom (*moving up* R *of the table*) Hi, Jude. (*He picks up the poker*) This thing's going to snap some day. (*He tries to straighten the poker*)

Isobel (*moving above the table*) Judy's been given the Student Award.

(Tom *struggles with the poker*)

Judy. Stop it. Put it down—you'll strain yourself.

B

Tom. *I've* not got blood pressure. (*By placing the poker against the edge of the table, he partially straightens it and holds it up*) Tarra! (*He hangs the poker on its hook and moves to* R *of the table*) Will you get paid?

Judy. Of course.

Tom. How much?

Judy. Seventy-five pounds.

Tom. Oh. Not bad.

Judy. If one of the big firms takes up my designs it'll be a lot more. Oliver Wentworth-Blake got the award the year before last. De Lissers took him up straight away, he gets three thousand a year.

(Isobel *and* Tom *look up at* Judy)

About three thousand, anyway. It was the only time it happened, it was exceptional.

Isobel. That's a lot of money.

Judy. Well, I'm not expecting anything like that. Oliver Wentworth-Blake's one of the top textile designers in the country. I'm not expecting—oh, I wish you wouldn't get so excited. (*She sits on the upstage end of the fender*)

Isobel (*her attitude to them quite tilted by the news*) D'you know, if we sold everything we've got we shouldn't have much more than three thousand pounds. (*She sits on the chair* L *of the table*)

Tom. Eh? The house, everything?

Isobel. Just about. (*She smiles at him rather anxiously*) How much did you think we'd got?

Tom. Does that include my Oxford money?

Isobel. It's not yours, Tom, but that includes it.

Tom. For God's sake, I thought he'd been making money.

Isobel. He's made enough to keep us all alive for twenty years.

Tom (*moving to the easy chair*) There are other ways of doing that. Why's he stuck it if they don't pay him?

Isobel (*uneasily*) They do pay him, of course.

Tom (*indicating the kitchen*) They can't pay him much. (*He sits on the right arm of the easy chair and faces Isobel*)

Isobel. Not a lot, no.

Judy. He likes the office.

Isobel. Don't be stupid, please.

Judy. He does; he likes it.

Isobel (*turning to look at them*) Judy, you keep your half-baked psychology for your own affairs.

Judy. Thank you.

Tom (*in support of Judy's theory*) Well, *I* don't get it.

Isobel. You? Why should you?

Tom. Why didn't he clear out?

(ISOBEL, *somewhat at bay against her own thoughts on the subject, uses her most violent weapon against Tom*)

ISOBEL. You'll understand one day—when you're grown up.
TOM. I won't, you know.
ISOBEL. So you think.
TOM. Damn it, you've only got one life.
ISOBEL. Oh, how *very* profound.
TOM. Well, do you think he did resign today?
JUDY (*indifferently*) What's this?
TOM. He says he's turned it in, but I don't believe it.
ISOBEL (*rising and moving down* C) How *dare* you!
JUDY. Oh, that. I agree with Tom. I'll believe it when I see it.
ISOBEL. You agree? If your father says he resigned, he resigned.
JUDY. Come off it, Mother.
ISOBEL. And what is that supposed to mean?
TOM. Well—come off it.
ISOBEL. I am speaking to Judy.
JUDY. I think you're being phoney, Mother.
TOM. Exactly. Do *you* believe it?
ISOBEL. Certainly I believe it. (*She moves up* C) Certainly I believe it. Your father wants to be a farmer. He hates the job; he's always wanted to be a farmer. You have no idea how much that means to him. He hates it and he's done it for you. For you, do you understand? He's a fine man. He's been through a great deal in all sorts of ways and you will treat him with respect. With respect! (*She sits on the chair* L *of the table*) With respect! With respect! (*She puts her face in her hands and weeps*)

(TOM *and* JUDY *regard her, guilty and embarrassed*)

TOM. Oh, Lord . . .
JUDY. Sorry, Mother.
TOM (*rising and moving to Isobel*) Yeh. Sorry.

(*There is a pause while* ISOBEL *weeps silently*)

JUDY. It isn't our fault.
TOM. Oh, shurrup, Judy.
JUDY. Well, facts are facts.
TOM (*inviting her to join his remorse*) It was a bit rough, though, all that.
JUDY. It's a bit tough on all of us.
TOM. "Rough" not "tough".
JUDY. "Rough", then.
TOM. Oh, shurrup.
JUDY (*shrugging*) Well. (*She collects her coat and bag*) I'll go and meet the bus.
ISOBEL. Just a minute. (*She wipes her nose*) I'm not at all sure about your taking a flat, Judy. I shall want to meet Carol first.

JUDY. I'm going for her now.

ISOBEL. And I shall have to discuss it with your father.

JUDY (*crossing to the door* R) Actually, Mother, we've pretty well decided.

(JUDY *exits* R)

TOM. Judy reacts all wrong. Are you O.K.?

ISOBEL. Yes. Yes. I'm O.K. Read your book.

TOM (*sitting in the easy chair*) Right. (*He reads for a moment*) Mum.

ISOBEL. Yes?

TOM. No. O.K.

(ISOBEL *looks round and laughs*)

ISOBEL. What is it, then?

TOM. Nothing really, I wonder what she's like.

ISOBEL. There's a photo on Judy's dressing-table.

TOM. Yeh, but it's touched up.

(*The front door bell rings*)

(*He rises and crosses to* R. *Eagerly*) Front door. I'll go. (*He pauses fractionally before the mirror*) Hell, Mum, I need a new shirt.

ISOBEL. There are two in your drawer. Go on—go to the door. (*She rises, pushes the chair into the table then moves up* C)

(TOM *exits* R. *Voices are heard off* R. ISOBEL *listens, curious. The voices cease*)

(*She calls*) Tom.

BOWMAN (*off; cheerfully*) Can I come in?

(DAVID BOWMAN *enters* R. *He is a tall active man in early middle age, with bird-like features and a countryman's complexion. His movements are slow and deft. Hatless, he wears a pepper-and-salt suit with bulging pockets. His expression is merry and determined. We see that Isobel is not what he expected. His manner becomes instantly more attentive*)

Good evening. Mrs Cherry?

ISOBEL (*wondering*) Yes. Good evening.

BOWMAN. The young man went upstairs.

ISOBEL. Oh, yes, my son . . .

BOWMAN (*moving to* R *of the table*) I've come to see your husband, but I understand he's not in.

ISOBEL. I shouldn't think he'd be long. Can I help?

BOWMAN. I don't know. May I sit down?

ISOBEL. Yes, of course. (*She moves up* R *of the table*) Is it about his work?

BOWMAN. I represent Stathams in the West Country.

ISOBEL (*cautiously*) Stathams.

BOWMAN. Yes. I'm the West Country rep, but I happened to be up today, and I thought I'd better come and see your husband personally. This is an awful time to call, by the way . . .

(TOM *enters* R)

TOM. Mother, where's my *green* shirt?
ISOBEL. Tom! Your green shirt's in the basket.

(TOM *crosses below the table to the laundry basket* L *of the dresser and searches in it.* BOWMAN *sits on the chair* R *of the table and takes a file of papers from his brief-case*)

I'm sorry he's not here. He would be normally. What do you want to see him about?
BOWMAN (*as one confirming the obvious*)   Oh, trees.
ISOBEL. Trees?
TOM. Apple trees?
BOWMAN. Yes. We're Stathams the growers. (*He takes a paper from his file*) This paper defeats me. We've been in correspondence with your husband for some time now, and as it's a biggish number of plants, I thought I'd like to meet him personally.

(TOM *moves to* L *of Isobel*)

Besides, I think your husband's making a mistake; he's thinking in terms of bush trees and I want to get him to consider half-standards . . .
ISOBEL. But . . .
BOWMAN. That isn't just sales talk, I honestly think it would be to his advantage. In the first place, he wouldn't need so many plants—it would cut the order by about seven hundred. The cost, of course, depends again. At the moment, he's talking of several rather fancy strains. (*He flips over a paper on the table*) Beauty of Bath, Sunset, Cornish Maiden, Egremont Russet, Farmer's Fortune, and so on; very nice fruit but all those aren't going to do well on the same soil, and most of them are . . .

(TOM *and* ISOBEL *exchange blank looks*)

(*He catches the exchange of looks, stops and laughs at his own enthusiasm*) Sorry—I'd better wait . . .
TOM. No, do go on, it's fascinating.
ISOBEL. Tom! I thought you wanted a shirt? (*She sits on the chair above the table*)

(TOM *returns to the laundry basket*)

Has Mr Cherry ordered these trees?
BOWMAN. Oh, not a firm order, but he obviously knows what he wants, and—(*he smiles*) well, I'm hoping to make a deal this evening. I hope he won't mind my calling, I couldn't let him

know because I wasn't sure I could make it this week. (*He consults another paper*)

(Tom *takes his green shirt from the basket, moves above the table and unbuttons the shirt he is wearing*)

Whereabouts in Somerset is this holding? He's sent us a sketch of the layout here; it looks a very good little property. I'm wondering what sort of soil you have.

(Tom *leans over Isobel*)

Isobel (*to Tom*) Will you go and put your shirt on in your bedroom, please?

(Tom *crosses below the table to the door* R)

I don't quite know what my husband has told you . . .
Bowman. Oh, nothing much; just that he wants to plant this property . . .
Isobel. We haven't got the property.
Bowman. Oh? (*He looks, puzzled, at the letters*)
Isobel. It—it's all rather in the air, you understand.
Bowman. Ah, the old story, eh? Right place, wrong price.

(Isobel *makes a non-committal gesture*)

Fifteen acres, isn't it?
Isobel (*reluctantly*) Yes.
Tom. Hey, I didn't know anything about this.
Isobel (*having forgotten him; furiously*) Is there any reason why you should?

(Tom *exits* R)

Look, Mr . . .?
Bowman. Oh. Bowman.
Isobel. Bowman—this enquiry of my husband's may not come to anything.
Bowman. Oh, we quite understand he's not made an order.
Isobel. No, but this place; we may never have it.
Bowman. Do you mind telling me what they're asking for it? (*He pauses*) Quite right; it's no business of mine.
Isobel (*liking him*) No, it's not that . . .
Bowman. I see you've got a southerly slope to two hundred feet? Is that the Quantocks, by any chance?
Isobel (*moving to the sink*) Really, I think it would be better to wait for my husband.
Bowman. Certainly.

(Isobel *turns and smiles at him*)

(*He rises and crosses to the easy chair. After a pause*) Well, it's a good life if you can take it.

(*They have entered into a confusion together and move about spasmodically, watching each other*)

And that's wonderful country down there.

ISOBEL. Yes. I don't know it myself but I've heard all about it; from my husband. It must be looking very fine, now.

BOWMAN. It will be in a week or two when the blossom's out. I like the town, though.

ISOBEL (*moving above the table*) Do you?

BOWMAN. Yes. It's nice to see people moving quickly for one thing. Down there everyone goes—(*with some exasperation*) one foot after another—at funeral pace.

ISOBEL. I suppose they can afford to.

BOWMAN. That's just what they can't if only they'd realize it. If you're in farming these days you're in business.

ISOBEL. What a pity.

BOWMAN (*politely*) Yes. (*He pauses*) I don't think I'd like to *live* in London. But I must say there's something about it. My wife loved it; she came from the town; she didn't like the country.

ISOBEL. Oh.

BOWMAN. Yes, I—we . . .

ISOBEL (*quickly*) The town's very expensive.

BOWMAN. My God, isn't it! (*He moves to the tray of cacti on the dresser and picks one up*) Whose is this?

ISOBEL. Oh, that's mine.

BOWMAN. Nice. Do you get flowers on this?

ISOBEL (*moving to R of Bowman*) Yes. (*She takes the cactus and replaces it*) There's the bud just coming up.

BOWMAN. What's it like?

ISOBEL (*touching her forehead*) Let me think. Oh, lovely. Yellow with bluey spots. Glorious! Rather horrible, really.

BOWMAN (*laughing*) Yes. You've got green fingers; I could never get mine to flower. (*He moves to the easy chair*) It's a good life if you pull together. I envy your husband, Mrs Cherry—he's on the right track.

ISOBEL (*moving down C*) Do you have an orchard?

BOWMAN. No—I like my job and I haven't got the money.

(TOM *enters* R *and stands down* R)

TOM. Hi!

ISOBEL. You look absolutely hideous.

TOM. What, this? The very thing!

BOWMAN. Look, if you can't buy this place, I could look out for something else for you.

ISOBEL. Well—er—my husband . . .

BOWMAN. Yes, of course, I'll mention it to him.

(TOM *moves up* R *of the table and looks at Bowman's papers*)

ISOBEL (*moving below the table*) I wonder if you'd mind waiting in the front room?

BOWMAN (*moving to L of Isobel*) No, of course not.

ISOBEL. Oh, your papers—Tom! (*She pushes Tom away*)

BOWMAN. Yes, thanks. (*He collects his papers and brief-case*)

ISOBEL (*picking up a magazine*) Would you like this?

BOWMAN (*taking the magazine*) Thanks, that's fine.

ISOBEL. There's an electric fire, I'll show you how to switch it on.

> (ISOBEL *exits* R.
> BOWMAN *catches* TOM's *eye, then follows Isobel off*)

(*Off*) And I'll tell my husband you're here as soon as he comes in.

BOWMAN (*off*) Yes, I expect we'll be able to sort it out between us.

ISOBEL (*off*) This is the room. There are some books.

> (*There is a slight pause.*
> ISOBEL *enters* R, *closes the door and looks at Tom*)

TOM (*facing Isobel*) Hey, Mum, is this on the level? Has he really left the . . .?

ISOBEL. You look like a little spiv. (*She crosses to the sink and puts the cauliflower in a saucepan*)

TOM (*following Isobel*) No, you don't get it. A spiv would look like a spiv, not me. It's a double take.

ISOBEL. Hideous.

TOM (*moving to the mirror and looking in it*) Very, very smart. A double take. (*He smooths his hair*) If she doesn't get it, she's dim (*He straightens his tie*) If she's dim, I can't use her. (*He crosses to the fender*)

ISOBEL (*taking the saucepan to the gas stove*) You're a sweet little thing. (*She puts the saucepan on the stove and lights the gas*)

TOM. Huh! So are you. (*He jerks his thumb towards the door* R) What gives with all this?

ISOBEL. For Heaven's sake, Tom, what does it matter to you?

TOM. I'm curious, that's all.

ISOBEL. Yes, well, stay curious.

> (CHERRY *enters* L, *comes into the kitchen, moves up* C, *throws his hat on to a chair and looks at Tom*)

CHERRY. Hello. Where's your barrow?

TOM (*not ready for another row, but keeping his end up*) Oh, down the road.

CHERRY (*rolling his sleeves and washing his hands at the sink*) What does he look like? (*He sniffs*) Do I smell cottage pie?

ISOBEL. Yes.

CHERRY. Not kept you, have I?

ISOBEL. No. It's in the oven.

CHERRY. The evenings are drawing out, aren't they?
ISOBEL. Yes.
CHERRY. Soon be Summer. Then Autumn. Then Christmas,
I suppose. (*He turns to face Isobel and dries his hands*) Well, now.

(ISOBEL *turns and looks at Cherry*)

(*He turns to gaze at Tom*) Where d'you say your barrow was?
How's trade?
TOM. Pretty brisk. I've been selling apples from your orchard.

(CHERRY, *drying his hands, turns his back on the others*)

CHERRY (*mildly and reasonably*)   I wonder what the significance
of *that* is supposed to be? I mean, apart from being a bit more of
your impudence, is it supposed to mean something?
TOM (*made awkward by Cherry's reasonable tone*)   Well, you began
it.
CHERRY (*turning to Tom*) Began what?
TOM (*now made silly*) You called me a barrow boy.
CHERRY. Good Lord, boy! That was only a bit of chaff; you'll
have to learn to take a ragging in the army. And you do look a
bit of a sight—to my way of thinking, anyway. (*He sits on the chair
above the table, picks up a magazine and opens it*) Still, every man to
his taste; you're old enough to dress yourself. (*His manner is of a
just but weary father*)
TOM (*defeated*) I'm going to get some cigarettes. (*He goes into
the garden*)
ISOBEL. Jim, I want to talk to you.

(CHERRY *catches* ISOBEL'*s eye, does not like it, rises and rapidly
pats his pocket*)

CHERRY. Just a jiffy, dear. (*He follows Tom into the garden*)
Tom! Tom! Get me an ounce of tobacco, will you? I seem to be
out. (*He takes a note from his wallet and hands it to Tom*)

(TOM *exits* L. ISOBEL *comes out on to the step*)

ISOBEL. Jim, there's a man here to see you; he's in the front
room.
CHERRY. Who is it?
ISOBEL. His name's Bowman.

(CHERRY *moves towards the kitchen*)

(*She restrains him*) I don't want him to hear.
CHERRY. Oh?
ISOBEL. From Stathams.
CHERRY. Oh, yes. (*Cheerfully*) Wonder what he wants?
ISOBEL. He wants to see you about some fruit trees.
CHERRY. Yes. I thought we could use half a dozen bushes in

the back, what d'you think? I thought I might train a nice peach against the wall of the coalhouse.

Isobel. He's talking in hundreds. He thinks you've got a farm in Somerset.

Cherry (*with a spluttering chuckle*) Me? Wish I had. (*He moves towards the door*) Better go and put him straight.

Isobel (*following Cherry*) Look, Jim . . . (*Hopelessly*) Ah, well . . . (*She moves down* L)

Cherry. What is it, dear?

Isobel (*in a spasm of anger*) You told him . . . You sent him a plan of it.

Cherry. Well, I just wanted to get an idea.

Isobel (*turning away and shaking her head*) Phooey!

Cherry. Now, don't take that tone, dear, I told him . . .

Isobel. Lies was what you told him.

Cherry (*moving down* R) I suppose I may write to a seedsman for some advice if I want to. I don't think we need a conference.

Isobel (*moving down and folding her arms*) Very well, what did you tell him?

Cherry. I'm not going to be cross-questioned about it, dear. I told him—it's some time ago . . . There's no harm in it.

Isobel. What kind of a fool does it make me look? I've been twenty minutes in there, twisting and dodging.

Cherry. I'm sorry for that, dear; you should have told him.

Isobel. What? That I'm married to an infant? That my husband's an idiot who lives in a seed catalogue? Oh, no, you tell him.

Cherry. All right, I will. (*He goes into the kitchen and crosses to the door* R)

Isobel (*following Cherry into the kitchen*) And tell him plainly. (*She closes the door and stands above the easy chair*) Finish it.

Cherry. Well, of course.

Isobel. "Of course." I don't want him back here. Tell him you haven't got an orchard.

Cherry. All right.

Isobel. Tell him there's no such place.

Cherry (*with dignity*) Very well. (*He pauses uncertainly at the door*)

Isobel. He's quite harmless. Go and tell him.

Cherry. I must say, Isobel, I resent——

Isobel (*moving up* L *of the table*) You didn't give in notice today, did you?

Cherry. —resent your tone.

Isobel. You didn't, did you?

Cherry. Oh, didn't I, though? You'll see at the end of the month.

Isobel. I don't want to see at the end of the month. I want to know if you gave in notice today.

CHERRY. You wouldn't need to ask if you'd been at the office. The whole office heard me. "You keep the job," I said, "I despise it." Straight from the shoulder.

ISOBEL. Jim! I want to know if you . . .

CHERRY (*moving up* R) Goddammit, I'm telling you. "Keep it," I said, "It's poisonous; it's unnatural; vile."

ISOBEL. You didn't, then.

CHERRY. By God, I don't know what more I could have said.

ISOBEL. You could have said, "Mr Burridge, I'm giving you a month's notice." Did you?

CHERRY. I said more than that.

ISOBEL (*disgusted*) Oh, Jim. (*She transfers Cherry's hat from the easy chair to the upstage end of the fender, then sits in the easy chair*)

CHERRY (*moving up* L) I'll say it before the month's out. Though I should have thought I'd made my feelings pretty plain today. I've had my bellyful of the Home Counties Insurance Society. (*He moves up* R) I'll say it tomorrow if that's what you want me to do.

ISOBEL. I don't want you to do anything.

CHERRY. Sorry, I thought you did.

ISOBEL. Yes, I suppose I do. But you can't do it.

CHERRY. Now, I won't have this damned hinting. (*He moves down* C) There may be this and that wrong, 'Bel, but for Heaven's sake let's be honest.

ISOBEL (*staring at him*) Honest! Jim, I think you must be a bit mad.

CHERRY. I shouldn't be surprised. (*He moves to the chair above the table and sits*) I'm not well, I know that. I had another turn today.

ISOBEL (*desperately*) No, Jim!

CHERRY. I did!

ISOBEL. Yes, but why mention it now?

CHERRY. Sorry. I thought you'd be interested.

ISOBEL. Well, I'm sorry, of course. You shouldn't drink so much. Especially that stuff.

CHERRY. I felt like ice from head to foot. I don't drink much.

ISOBEL. I expect you've had three or four pints since you came in.

CHERRY. There you go, you see. I haven't had anything like four pints. Anyway, what's four pints of scrumpy?

ISOBEL (*shrugging*) They're your arteries.

CHERRY (*coaxing*) Eh, 'Bel. (*He rises*) Cheer up, eh? (*He sits on the right arm of the easy chair*) Come on, 'Bel.

ISOBEL (*wearily*) Yes, sure. Only tell this Bowman the truth, eh? Just for once tell the truth. You haven't got an orchard; you never will have an orchard.

CHERRY. Don't be too sure about that. Orr, you make too much of things, 'Bel.

(*The music of the "Flowering Cherry" theme is heard*)

I shall need this chap one day. All right, you'll see, one day I'll surprise you, one Spring I'll surprise you, "Come on," I'll say, "come and see what we've got," and we'll leave the kids and drive down there. Then you'll see, 'Bel, a hundred trees in a row, and thirty rows—Egremont, Cornish Maiden, Farmer's Fortune, all in blossom, meeting over your head; it does, it meets over your head in a standard orchard; you can't see anything but blossoms. By God, 'Bel, you'll see—that's the day I'm living for.

(*The music fades*)

(*He wags his finger at her*) And it may not be so far round the corner.

(ISOBEL *looks flatly at him, exhausted, but manages a helpless shrug and a smile*)

ISOBEL (*rising*) It's a nice dream, Jim. (*She crosses above the easy chair and table to the gas stove*)

CHERRY. Now, why a dream? (*He rises*)

ISOBEL. A nice, innocent dream; as a dream it's fine.

CHERRY (*moving to* L *of the easy chair*) You know what they say: you've got to have one.

ISOBEL. They're right, too.

CHERRY (*impressed*) By Jingo, you sound fed up.

ISOBEL (*smiling coldly*) No dream.

CHERRY. O-o-h, tell that to the Marines.

ISOBEL. I haven't.

CHERRY (*roguishly*) No? Venice? (*He sits on the left arm of the easy chair and faces up stage*) The little house by the Rialto? With the balcony and the yellow canvas awning?

ISOBEL (*genuinely surprised*) Good Lord! (*A little moved by this voice from the past, but sensible*) I'd forgotten that.

CHERRY. Ha! Well, I hadn't. We'll spend the Winter in Venice. As soon as the picking's over and the crop's marketed, we'll leave Somerset . . .

ISOBEL. But we're not in Somerset. Or Venice. Or the moon or the morning star. (*She sits on the chair above the table*) This is where we live.

CHERRY (*clinging to his whimsy*) Not for always.

ISOBEL. For the last twenty-five years. (*Earnestly*) The middle cut Cherry. I was twenty when we came here. And now what? The Prime of Life? I don't think so. (*She sees that she has at last caught the centre of his attention and falls gratefully into simple personalness*) How long—how long is it since we . . .?

CHERRY. What?

ISOBEL. Slept together.

CHERRY. Eh?

ISOBEL. How long?

CHERRY (*rising and facing front; alarmed*) Dash it all, Isobel. We're not newlyweds.

ISOBEL. No, but I'm just asking how long. Do you know?

CHERRY (*looking away*) Yes.

ISOBEL. It's a long time.

CHERRY. Damnation, *you* didn't . . .

ISOBEL. That's true.

CHERRY. It's not all that important.

ISOBEL. It is.

(*There is a silence*)

CHERRY. I did have a row with Burridge today, but the boot was on the other foot. He was shouting at me.

ISOBEL. I wish you *had* done it.

CHERRY. *You* do? You don't.

ISOBEL. I don't know. It'd be something definite.

CHERRY. It'd be definite all right.

ISOBEL. That's all I want.

CHERRY (*after a pause*) It's coming to a head between us, isn't it, 'Bel?

ISOBEL. Yes, Jim, I think it is.

CHERRY (*not exclaiming; quietly*) Ah, Christ, I'm sorry, 'Bel. (*He sits on the downstage end of the fender*)

ISOBEL. This is my dream, Jim, if you want it. To have you come home on time and us have tea together, and half an hour's talk without a single lie, or even half a lie; and a straight look from here—(*she touches her eye, then points to Cherry*) to there. And none of this glancing and winking and looking away. And then wash up together and no-one leave any dirty bits for anyone else.

(CHERRY *commences a gesture of guilt*)

(*She rises, moves down* C *and faces him*) No, no, I mean for both of us, for both of us. And then—go to the pictures if we want to, not if we don't, and anything—have a row if we want a row, really want a real row, and then if we want to make love— (*gently*) if we want to . . . Only no more cardboard prospects.

CHERRY. Yes, well, I deserved that.

ISOBEL. No, no—not like that.

CHERRY. No, but that's me all right, I'd better pull myself together. I could do that job left-handed—left-handed. (*Wryly*) I'll apologize to Burridge tomorrow.

ISOBEL. What was the row about?

(TOM *enters* R.

CAROL *follows him on. She is one of those people who win raffles; with her, good luck is almost an attribute, almost visible. She is a natural, sun-happy, even in London. She bestows ad lib. a friendliness which costs her nothing. In appearance, complexion, hair, clothes, she is tawny, as though straight from a beach. She is athletic but*

cuddlesome. She has a big warm smile and splendid teeth. She finds
pleasure as water finds its level but like water, can be decisive when she
finds herself restrained. When she has had her run as a girl, she is
going to make someone a remarkably unfaithful wife)

Tom (*grinning*) Mother, this is Carol. (*He stands behind Carol*)
Carol (*smiling*) Hello.
Isobel (*smiling*) Hello, Carol. (*She crosses and shakes hands*) How
are you?
Carol. I'm fine, thanks.
Isobel. My, you look fine. Have you been on holiday?
Carol. No.
Cherry (*rising; smiling*) She's a country girl.
Carol (*indignantly*) I'm not.

(*The others laugh*)

Tom (*gracefully, he too wants the family to appear well*) This is
my father.

(Carol *crosses to Cherry and shakes hands with him.* Tom *moves
below the table and leans on it*)

Cherry. How d'you do, my dear?
Carol. Good evening. I hope I'm not late?
Cherry. If you are, it's your prerogative.
Carol. I don't carry the time.
Cherry. Very sensible. I wish I didn't. Ha ha!

(Cherry *and* Carol *stand and smile at one another*)

Isobel. Jim, are you going to see Mr Bowman?
Cherry (*easily*) Oh, yes. A little matter of business to attend
to. You're not going, I hope?
Carol. No, I don't think so.
Cherry (*crossing to the door* R) I'll be seeing you, then. (*To
Isobel, for Carol's benefit, with assurance*) I'll just settle this chap.

(Cherry *exits* R. Isobel *looks after him*)

Tom. I found her in the road.
Isobel (*turning*) Where's Judy?
Tom. Oh, Lord!
Carol. Judy?
Isobel. You don't mean to say you left her . . .

(Judy *enters* L *and comes into the kitchen*)

Judy. Hello.
Carol. Hello, Judy.
Judy (*to Carol*) I've been waiting at the bus stop.
Carol. For me?
Judy. That's what we arranged. Did you forget?

CAROL (*crossing to* R *of Judy*) I'm awfully sorry, darling. We went out and they got me a taxi.

JUDY. Gosh! Who?

CAROL (*a shade resentful of Judy's tone*) Peter and Wilfred got the taxi.

(TOM *rises and moves up* L *of the table*)

JUDY. Was anyone else there?

CAROL (*a shade more resentful*) Yes; Suzie and Elspeth and Johnny Idasalski.

JUDY. What did you do?

CAROL. We went to the pictures. *Clair de Lune.* (*Coolly*) You've seen it.

JUDY. I wouldn't have minded seeing it again.

(ISOBEL *moves up* R)

(*Moderating*) This is my mother.

CAROL. Yes, Tom just introduced me.

(TOM *sits on the upstage side of the table*)

JUDY. Oh. (*More gently*) Would you like to take your coat off?

CAROL. Thanks. (*She removes her coat*)

(TOM *has been sitting on the table but now is off it like a shot and helps* CAROL. *He takes her coat and hangs it outside the door* R. *It transpires that* CAROL's *arms and throat are of the same golden brown. The others look at her.* ISOBEL *shuffles out of her slippers and into a pair of court shoes*)

ISOBEL. Well. (*She moves down and faces Carol*) So this is Carol.

CAROL. I'm afraid so.

(ISOBEL *laughs protestingly and lays a hand on Carol's arm*)

ISOBEL. Oh, there's nothing to be afraid of. Have you eaten? (*She moves to the stove and looks in the oven*)

CAROL. Yes, thanks.

JUDY. Oh, Carol, you are awful. She hasn't, Mummy. I know she hasn't. She's slimming.

ISOBEL (*straightening up*) Don't make her eat, Judy. (*She sees her reflection in the mirror behind the gas stove and falls to examining herself despondently*)

TOM. It's cottage pie. Pretty good.

CAROL. Well, I'll have some if it'll go round. (*She sits in the easy chair*)

(JUDY *removes her coat and puts it on the laundry basket*)

TOM (*moving down* R *of the table*) How did you like *Clair de Lune?*

CAROL. I thought it was rather corny, you know.

TOM. *Le mot juste! C'est* exàct! Corny. (*He moves to the chair* L *of the table, sits, gives Carol a cigarette, takes one for himself and lights them*)

CAROL.   Everything so terribly significant all the time.

TOM. And so *dated*.

CAROL. Well, yes, it *is* dated.

TOM. Oh, the French have gone down the nick.

(JUDY *picks up Cherry's hat, drops it on the floor, then sits on the upstage end of the fender*)

JUDY. It's all that other stuff I can't stand.

CAROL. What?

JUDY. All that sexy stuff.

CAROL. That's what I find pretty hard to take.

JUDY. That man was old enough to be her . . . He was a completely different generation.

(ISOBEL *moves to* R *of the table and smooths the cloth*)

CAROL (*without much interest*)   Yes.

JUDY. You could see all the little marks on his face.

TOM (*without much interest*)   Mm. Oh, it was corny, all right.

ISOBEL. I thought it was a very good film.

CAROL (*surprised*)   Have you seen it?

ISOBEL. Well, yes, there's no age limit.

TOM. What was so good about it?

ISOBEL. It was gentle.

CAROL (*regarding Isobel*)   That's true.

TOM. Oh, there were some good bits in it.

CAROL. That scene in the Sunday School was gentle. It got me all right.

ISOBEL (*after a glance in the mirror; decisively*)   Judy, I'm going upstairs. Turn the oven off if I'm not down. (*She moves to the door* R) I look a fright.

(ISOBEL *exits* R)

CAROL (*as Isobel goes*)   Oh, you don't . . . (*To Judy*) Your mother's a real person.

JUDY. She's a very intelligent woman.

CAROL. She's good-looking, isn't she? You ought to make her dress properly.

JUDY. She isn't interested in that.

CAROL. Really? What about your father? Frighteningly masculine, I thought.

TOM. No, he's a phoney.

CAROL. Are you sure?

TOM. He was decorated in the Great War.

JUDY. Joined up as a boy.

TOM. All that . . .

Judy. But even so . . .

Tom. Oh, yes. He's a phoney. Unquestionably.

Judy. I can't think why she married him.

Tom. There's nothing to him. Mind you, the 'twenties—they were all half batty, anyway.

Judy. She ought to have married someone completely different.

Carol. Who?

Judy. Someone of her own intellectual level.

Tom. Nah, that's not it.

Carol (*lazily with curiosity*) Judy, do you hate your father?

Judy. No, I don't hate him—no.

Carol. I wonder if this is why your work's so good?

Tom. She's good, is she?

Carol. Haven't you told them?

Judy. Yes. Don't start talking about it.

Tom. Oh. the Student Award; yes, terrific, isn't it?

Judy. For Heaven's sake, what does it matter?

Isobel (*off upstairs; calling indistinctly*) Judy!

(Judy *rises, crosses to the door* R, *opens it and calls*)

Judy. Yes?

Isobel (*off*) Judy, have you still got that lipstick I like? The pinky one?

Judy. It's in the top left-hand drawer of my dressing-table.

Isobel (*off*) Dressing-table?

Judy. Yes.

Isobel (*off*) Top left-hand . . .?

Judy. Wait a minute. I'm coming.

(Judy *exits* R. Tom *rises, takes the ashtray from the table and puts it on the arm of Carol's chair*)

Tom. So it turns out that Judy knows her stuff?

Carol. Oh, yes. She'll be earning four figures before she's much older.

Tom. Go on? She's nutty about you.

Carol. Me?

Tom. You going to show her around a bit? She doesn't get round enough, I don't think.

Carol. Golly, *I* don't know.

Tom. I bet you do, though.

(Carol *picks up* Tom's *book*)

Carol (*with a demure catlike smile*) Who's reading Eliot?

Tom (*taking the book from Carol and moving up* c) I am. Pretty corny, really. (*After a pause. Excitedly*) Could you stand the flicks again, this evening?

Carol. Why not?

Tom. Good. That's—good.

c

CAROL (*laughing softly at him*) You're going into the army, aren't you?

TOM. Yes. (*He sits on the right arm of the easy chair*) I don't want to.

CAROL. Will you get a commission?

TOM. Oh, I expect so.

(JUDY *enters* R *and moves below the table*)

JUDY (*over her shoulder*) It's all right, Mother. Carol will have one.

(ISOBEL *enters* R)

ISOBEL. No, don't, Judy.

CAROL. What?

JUDY. Mother wants a pink lipstick.

ISOBEL. It really doesn't matter. Really.

CAROL (*looking in her bag*) Yes, I've got one—I think. Yes— (*she takes a lipstick from her bag*) here it is.

ISOBEL. Oh, it doesn't matter a bit. (*Briskly*) Come on, Judy: knives, forks, two spoons each. (*She moves the chair above the table towards the left end, then collects the chair from below the gas stove and puts it above the right end of the table*)

(JUDY *clears the magazines from the table on to the table* R, *then crosses to the dresser*)

Tom! *Tom*, table mats.

TOM. Right! (*He goes to the dresser, collects the table mats and puts them on the table*)

(*A to-ing and fro-ing breaks out as the table is spread and laid with crockery and cutlery, in a familiar domestic dance, but today with a counter-point of aroused vanity because of Carol*)

CAROL (*rising and crossing to Isobel*) No, look, do use it. (*She offers the lipstick*)

JUDY. Big spoons?

ISOBEL. What a lovely pink. (*To Judy*) One soup, one fruit. (*To Carol*) May I? (*She takes the lipstick and goes to the mirror* R)

CAROL. What can I do?

TOM. I dunno. Draw some cider—shall we have cider, Mum?

ISOBEL. Not for me, dear.

JUDY. Nor me, thank you. (*She brings knives, forks, spoons, pepper and salt pots to the table and sets them out*)

TOM (*moving to the dresser*) That's one—two—(*he hands two glasses to Carol*)

CAROL. Mr Cherry?

TOM (*handing a mug to Carol*) —and three's a crowd. Barrel's over here.

(TOM *and* CAROL *cross to the barrel*)

JUDY. There's no salt in the salt cellar.

(CAROL *fiddles with the tap on the barrel*)

TOM. No! Not like that, you've turned it off. Look. (*He turns on the tap*)

CAROL (*filling the glass*) Oh, I get it.

JUDY. These soup spoons are dirty.

TOM (*moving up* C) Well, polish them. (*He tosses a tea towel to Judy*) Where are the other mats? (*He moves to the dresser*)

ISOBEL. In the cardboard box at the back.

(CAROL *turns off the tap and puts the glass of cider on the table.* TOM *takes some mats from the dresser drawer*)

JUDY. Not those, they're disgusting.

TOM (*holding up the mats*) Hand painted in the heart of—guess where? Somerset! (*He puts the mats on the table*) Family joke.

CAROL. Oh.

ISOBEL (*turning from the mirror*) No, it's too young.

CAROL. It isn't. Is it?

TOM. No—just the job.

JUDY. It's very nice, Mother.

(TOM *wolf whistles*)

ISOBEL. Well, I don't know, I'm sure. (*She hands the lipstick to Carol*) Thank you. (*She sets out the mats on the table*) How are you getting on?

(CAROL *fills the second glass with cider*)

TOM. Fine. We could use some new mats.

ISOBEL. These are practically new.

JUDY. And there's no salt in the salt cellar. (*She takes the salt cellar to the dresser and fills it*)

ISOBEL. I like your slacks, Carol.

CAROL. Do you really?

ISOBEL. Mmm.

CAROL. Forty-five shillings.

ISOBEL. Never!

CAROL. It's a fact. I'll give you the address.

ISOBEL. Me? Now, if you know a good place for little lace shawls . . . (*She takes the glass from Carol and puts it on the table*)

(JUDY *puts the salt cellar on the table and hangs up the tea cloth*)

CAROL. No, you're *just* the kind of person that ought to wear trews.

ISOBEL. Well, it's very nice of you to say so. Mr Cherry will draw his own. (*She takes the pan from the gas stove to the sink and strains off the water*)

(CAROL *puts the mug on the table.* JUDY *stands above the easy chair*)

TOM. Judy, Carol wants to go to the flicks. (*He stands up* C)

CAROL (*crossing and sitting in the easy chair*) I should mention I'm flat broke.

TOM. I'll take care of that. How about it, Judy?

JUDY (*sitting on the upstage end of the fender*) Whose idea was that?

CHERRY (*off* R) So what does Jesse do? He gets both his shoulders right under her belly——

(CHERRY *enters* R, *holds the door open and looks back*)

—gives a tremendous·heave—and walks into the yard with the horse on his back. (*He moves down* R)

(BOWMAN *enters* R, *closes the door and stands up* R. TOM *crosses and sits on the floor below the fender*)

BOWMAN (*politely*) Ha! What did your father do?

CHERRY. Couldn't do anything. "'Ere she be, gaffer," says Jesse, "I toald 'ee 'ee'd bought a cripple."

BOWMAN (*glancing at Isobel*) Good Lord!

(ISOBEL *puts the saucepan on the draining board*)

CHERRY (*moving above the table*) Oh, he—he was a character. (*He looks at the table*) But you haven't set a place for my good friend, Mr Bowman.

BOWMAN. Oh, I can't possibly . . .

ISOBEL (*expressionless*) Will you stop to supper, Mr Bowman?

BOWMAN. There's nothing I should like better, but . . .

CHERRY. That's right.

BOWMAN (*rather sharply*) I really can't. I should have started home an hour ago.

CHERRY. Well, then, well . . . Ah! (*To Isobel*) D'you know where my grafting knife is, darling? Mr Bowman's going to have it sharpened for me.

ISOBEL (*moving to the dresser*) Yes, I think so. (*She takes the knife from the dresser drawer*)

(CHERRY *grabs the knife*)

Can't the ironmonger do it?

CHERRY (*crossing to Bowman*) That's the item, Squire.

BOWMAN. Oh, yes. An ironmonger could do it, you know.

CHERRY. Now, you give it to your man and let him make a proper job of it—if it's not too much trouble, that is.

BOWMAN. Not at all.

CHERRY. You know what it is: you show that to these chaps up here, never seen one before.

(BOWMAN *takes the knife*)

(*He crosses to the barrel*) Now, a jar of scrumpy before you go?

BOWMAN. No, thank you, I've a long way to drive.

CHERRY. Wish I was coming with you. Still, there it is, then. I won't detain you.

BOWMAN (*crossing to Isobel*)   Good night, Mrs Cherry.

ISOBEL. Good night.

CHERRY (*leading Bowman to the door* L)   This way. It's quicker. And I'll think about what you say.

BOWMAN. Good.

(CHERRY *and* BOWMAN *go into the garden*)

CHERRY. I'm not convinced, mind you. I was brought up in a different school—bushes or standards, I was taught . . . Well, cheerio, old man. It's been delightful meeting you. I'll see you some time soon?

(ISOBEL *picks up the saucepan and puts it on the stove*)

BOWMAN. Er, yes.

CHERRY. We'll make an evening of it.

BOWMAN. Yes, we will. Good-bye.

(BOWMAN *exits* L)

CHERRY (*calling*)   Good-bye, old man. *Bon voyage.* (*He goes into the kitchen and stands up* C) Delightful chap, isn't he?

ISOBEL. Is he coming back?

(CHERRY *picks up one of the glasses of cider and holds it to the light*)

CHERRY. Oh, oh, oh. Who drew the cider?

CAROL. I did. (*Winsomely*) Isn't it all right?

CHERRY (*wagging his finger at her*)   You don't come from Somerset.

CAROL. No, I don't.

CHERRY. Now, you come here and I'll show you.

(CAROL *rises.* CHERRY *takes* CAROL's *hand, leads her to the barrel, puts his finger over the spigot, then picks up the mug.* CAROL *stands above the barrel*)

Now. You put your finger over the spigot, like this . . .

(ISOBEL *moves to the dresser and collects some plates.* TOM *rises.* JUDY *rises and stands above the easy chair*)

CAROL. Mine isn't big enough. (*She shows him*)

CHERRY (*charmed*)   Good Heavens above, look at this child's hand. What's that good for?

CAROL. Nothing.

CHERRY. Ha, ha! Well, if you can find someone with fingers like cucumbers, you can tell him this is the way to draw cider. (*He fills the mug*) See?

CAROL (*with great interest*)   Oh, yes.

CHERRY. See?

TOM. Makes you wonder what they'll invent next, doesn't it?

CHERRY. Don't ask *him* to do it, mind. He'd get sucked through and drowned.

ISOBEL. Supper's ready. (*She moves above the table*)

(CAROL *crosses and sits in the easy chair.* TOM *sits on the upstage end of the fender*)

CHERRY. Are the plates hot?

ISOBEL. No, I forgot.

CHERRY (*grabbing the plates and putting them in the oven*) Must have hot plates for Shepherd's Pie.

(CHERRY *is about to rejoin the children but* ISOBEL *detains him. Meanwhile* CAROL *sits opposite* TOM *and they mime their own conversation as follows.* CAROL *speaks to* TOM, *who sulkily replies.* CAROL *sits right forward on her chair, flattering him.* JUDY *picks up* TOM'*s book and stands* R *of him. The three of them put their heads together and talk animatedly over the book,* TOM *rehabilitating himself*)

ISOBEL. Jim.

CHERRY. Hello?

ISOBEL. Is he coming back?

CHERRY. I suppose so.

ISOBEL. Why?

CHERRY. Well, he's got my knife, hasn't he?

ISOBEL. He's coming all the way from Somerset with your knife?

CHERRY. No, of course not.

ISOBEL. Jim, *did* you tell him?

CHERRY (*crossing to the easy chair; irritably*) Tell him what?

(ISOBEL *looks malevolently at Cherry*)

TOM (*reading*)
Do I dare
Disturb the universe?
In a minute there is time
For decisions and revisions which a minute will reverse.

For I have known them all already, known them all—
Have known the evenings, mornings, afternoons,
I have measured out my life with coffee spoons; . . .

CHERRY. With what?

JUDY. Coffee spoons.

CHERRY. Blimey! (*He winks at Carol*) Well, go on.

(TOM *rises, sighs, closes the book and puts it on the fender*)

TOM. Let's go and eat. (*He moves above the left end of the table*)

(CAROL *rises.* CHERRY *leads* CAROL *to the chair above the right end of the table, where she sits.* ISOBEL *goes to the dresser and gets some tea spoons from the drawer*)

CAROL. Did that man really carry a horse on his back?

CHERRY. He did, my dear. (*He sits* R *of the table*)

CAROL. Hell, he must have been strong.

TOM (*with satirical awe*) He was so strong, he could bend that poker.

CAROL. Crikey!

(JUDY *picks up* TOM'S *book, then sits on the chair below the table*)

TOM (*sitting above the left end of the table*) You'll enjoy the film tonight. It's full of hairy Marines.

CAROL. Good-oh.

JUDY (*giggling*) Carol, you are terrible.

CHERRY. Going to the pictures?

TOM (*anxiously*) Yes.

CHERRY (*lofty and shrewd*) Er, have you got my tobacco, Tom?

(TOM *rises, takes a packet of tobacco from his pocket, hands it to Cherry and looks anxiously at him*)

Thank you—and the change?

(ISOBEL *looks sharply and alarmed at* TOM, *who confusedly digs in his pockets*)

Oh, d'you need it?

TOM. Well . . .

CHERRY. That's all right, lad, keep it—only—mustn't forget to ask, you know.

(TOM *looks at* ISOBEL, *meets her angry glance and is further confused*)

TOM (*muttering*) Thank you. (*He resumes his seat*)

CHERRY. Yes, this man, Carol . . . (*He rises and takes the thinner poker from the hook*)

(ISOBEL *sits on the chair* L *of the table*)

Hello! Who straightened this?

TOM (*gladly*) I did.

CHERRY. *You* did? You must have used your feet.

TOM. No, I didn't—I did it on the edge of the table.

CHERRY. Aha! (*He straightens the poker fully*)

CAROL. Gosh! Can you do the big one?

CHERRY (*replacing the poker*) No. No-one in—(*contemptuously*) London could. (*He resumes his seat* R *of the table*) I might if I'd been doing the job I was born to. (*Significantly*) You come down to Somerset in a year's time and I might be able to show you something.

CAROL (*playing up*) Oh?

CHERRY. Yes, I—well, let's just say I've taken certain steps today, to terminate my present sedentary occupation.

ISOBEL (*rising*) Oh—Jim! (*She runs swiftly out to the garden and leans against the trellis*)

CHERRY (*rising and moving up* C; *startled*) Where you going, 'Bel? (*To the others. With forced comic surprise*) Where's she gone?

JUDY. Read us some more, Tom.

CAROL. He reads well, doesn't he?

JUDY. Yes, he does.

CHERRY. What, more coffee spoons? That's not poetry. (*He moves up* R) "Oh, for a muse of fire . . ."

TOM. Go on, then.

CHERRY. D'you think I can't? Eh?

TOM. All right, if you can.

CHERRY. He thinks he's the only man in England that knows any poetry.

TOM. All right, go on, then.

(CHERRY *recites in a powerful, deep and fluent voice, circling the table and easy chair as he speaks*)

CHERRY (*with emotion*)
"Oh, for a muse of fire that would ascend
 The brightest heaven of invention,
 A kingdom for a stage, princes to act,
 And monarchs to behold the swelling scene!
 Then should the warlike Harry, like himself,
 Assume the port of Mars; . . ."

CAROL (*moved to genuine admiration*) Pretty good!

(ISOBEL, *in the garden, unhearing, leaning against the trellis, throws her head back and cries exhaustedly*)

CHERRY. Wait a tick.

"Assume the port of Mars; and at his heels,
 Leash'd in like hounds, . . ."
 (*He picks up the big poker*)

ISOBEL. Oh, let me, let me, let me leave him.

CHERRY.
"Should famine, sword, and fire.
 Crouch for employment. . . ."

ISOBEL. Give me the strength; just for a moment.

CHERRY.
"But pardon, gentles all . . ."

ISOBEL. Just for long enough to walk out.

CHERRY.
  "B t pardon . . ."

ISOBEL. To get away from him. To get away from him for good.

CHERRY.
  "But pardon . . ."

ISOBEL. Oh, let me, let me, let me leave.

CHERRY.
  "But pardon, gentles all . . ."

 The lights dim to BLACK-OUT *as—*

    the CURTAIN *falls*

ACT II

SCENE—*The same. One month later. Afternoon.*

When the CURTAIN *rises, the stage is empty. A clock chimes four.* CHERRY *enters quietly* L, *crosses to the kitchen door, hesitates, places his hand on the door-knob, consults his wrist-watch then hesitates again. He looks through the key-hole, braces himself, and opens the door with a manner which will look normally assured if there is someone in the kitchen, but which makes no noise. Once inside, his step is stealthy but urgent. He quietly closes the door, crosses to the door* R, *listens a moment, then goes to the dresser. He quickly opens a drawer, looks in it, closes it and opens another. He takes Isobel's handbag from the drawer, turns and puts it on the table. He takes two one-pound notes from the bag, puts them in his wallet then replaces the bag in the drawer. He is trembling. His glance falls on the cider barrel. He hesitates, looks at the door, then gets his mug from the dresser, goes to the barrel and draws a mug of cider. He takes a small bottle of gin from his pocket, laces the drink heavily with gin, replaces the bottle in his pocket and drinks. He leans on the chair* R *of the table, tipping it slightly. Then he straightens up, the bang of the chair startles him, and he glances uneasily around. Silence prevails. He relaxes slightly; he is at the same time trying to think and using the drink to protect him from what he has to think about. There is a spray of apple blossom in a clean milk bottle on the table. He is about to drink again when he sees the blossom; he puts down the mug, approaches his face, and draws it across the petals, thinking. The rattle of the letterbox is heard off* R, *followed by the postman's knock. He cocks his head sharply.* ISOBEL *is heard off in the distance, calling.* CHERRY *is about to go out to the garden, sees his mug on the table, darts back for it and is about to go again.*

ISOBEL (*off; calling*) Tom?

(CHERRY *is too late. He spins his hat on to the easy chair and assumes a nonchalant pose.*

ISOBEL *enters* R. *She carries some letters*)

Jim! What time is it?

CHERRY (*consulting his watch*) I'm playing hookey.

ISOBEL (*this is evidently not the first time*) You've been coming home early a lot lately. (*She stands above the table*) Don't get into trouble again.

CHERRY. Cat's away, you know.

ISOBEL. Is old Burridge still on holiday?

CHERRY. Yes, he is.

ISOBEL. You are getting on much better with him now, aren't you?

38

CHERRY. Oh, yes. Anything in the post?

ISOBEL. Oh. (*She hands a letter to Cherry*) There's an Army letter for Tom. D'you think that's it?

CHERRY. *I* don't know. (*He puts the letter on the table*)

ISOBEL. Jim, do you think he'll be all right?

CHERRY. He'll be fine. A credit to you.

ISOBEL (*pleased*) Really?

CHERRY. Sure of it. He is already. They both are.

ISOBEL (*sitting on the chair above the table*) It's nice to have you home so early.

CHERRY (*sitting on the left arm of the easy chair*) Nice to *be* home early.

ISOBEL (*smiling at him*) Jim, I think we're all right.

CHERRY. Oh, yes. (*He rises, picks up his hat and puts it on the upstage end of the fender*)

ISOBEL. Let's drink to it. (*She reaches for Cherry's glass*)

CHERRY (*alarmed*) Hey! (*He moves to Isobel and snatches up his glass. Jokingly*) Hands off my scrumpy!

ISOBEL. My!

CHERRY (*collecting a glass from the dresser*) Let me get you one. (*He crosses to the barrel and fills the glass with cider*) No, you know, I never like anyone drinking my scrumpy.

ISOBEL. Don't fill it, Jim.

CHERRY (*handing the glass to Isobel*) Well, here's to us, eh?

ISOBEL. May our dreams come true.

CHERRY. Right!

ISOBEL. I don't mean Venice, you know. I mean—us. Oh, well, anyway. Cheers!

CHERRY. Cheers!

(*They drink*)

ISOBEL (*putting down her glass; with a little grimace*) I hope you're right about Tom. I don't think his character's at all formed yet.

CHERRY (*sitting R of the table; heavily*) If it isn't, Heaven knows it isn't *your* fault, that's all I can say.

ISOBEL (*touched; protesting*) Or yours, Jim.

CHERRY (*wriggling; unconsciously feeling these to be coals of fire*) Well, I—hope not, of course.

ISOBEL. Oh, dear. (*She looks at her letters*) More bills. (*She pauses*) This girl Carol. Do you think she's attractive?

CHERRY (*too loudly*) Attractive?

ISOBEL. I do.

CHERRY. She's got a nice nature.

ISOBEL. I wonder about that. These last few weeks since Tom's been seeing her—she makes him greedy. (*She opens a letter*) Oh, dear. This is the third reminder. I'd better go round and pay. (*She rises, moves to the dresser and opens the drawer*)

CHERRY. What is it?

ISOBEL. Coal and coke. (*She looks in the drawer*) Do you know where my bag is? (*She searches*)

CHERRY (*fascinated as Isobel searches*) No.

ISOBEL (*opening the other drawer*) I think she's good for Judy— or is she? (*She takes her handbag from the drawer and moves to the table*)

CHERRY. Let me write you a cheque.

ISOBEL. No, it's only thirty-four shillings. (*She looks in her handbag*) I don't think Judy's all that plain, do you?

CHERRY (*watching helplessly*) No. A little awkward, perhaps. Over-fastidious.

(ISOBEL *turns to the light and takes out her purse. Her figure grows tense*)

(*Desperately*) I think Judy's over-fastidious, 'Bel.

(ISOBEL *rummages quickly in her purse*)

Fastidious . . .

ISOBEL. O-o-o-oh, *God!*

CHERRY. What's up?

ISOBEL (*sitting above the table*) I must make sure. (*She searches resolutely in her bag, then puts it on the table. Dejected*) No. Gone.

(CHERRY *stares in silence*)

Tom's stealing again.

CHERRY. Are you sure it's not there?

ISOBEL. Perfectly.

CHERRY. How much are you missing?

ISOBEL. Two pounds.

CHERRY. Notes?

ISOBEL. Yes.

CHERRY. You may have lost them.

ISOBEL. No. They've been taken from my bag. It's Tom.

CHERRY. Yes, I suppose so. (*Uncomfortably*) Must it be Tom?

ISOBEL. Who else? Who needs to?

CHERRY. You perhaps left it somewhere?

ISOBEL. I'm afraid not, Jim. He took some last week.

CHERRY (*covering surprise with a dead-pan expression*) Last week?

ISOBEL. Two ten-shilling notes. And now two pounds. Oh, it's so disgusting. Why can't he ask for it? I thought we were past all this. What *is* going to become of the boy? Well, you'll have to lend it me now, Jim. D'you mind? Just a couple.

CHERRY. Cheque no good, eh? (*He takes his wallet from his pocket*) There we are, then. (*He hands the two notes to Isobel, laughs, then displays his empty wallet*)

ISOBEL. Oh, I've cleaned you out. I thought I might be wrong about it last week, but . . . (*She rises and puts her bag in the dresser drawer*) Oh, Jim, if we're going to *steal* from one another . . .

CHERRY. Now, Isobel, be careful. You may be mistaken.

ISOBEL. There's no mistake, dear. I marked the notes.

CHERRY. Marked them?

ISOBEL (*putting the notes in her pocket*) Yes. That's the state we're reduced to. (*She sits above the table*) Wherever those notes are, they're marked.

(TOM *enters* L, *crosses the garden and comes into the kitchen*)

TOM. Hello. Hello—you're home early, Dad. (*The atmosphere hits him*) Uh?

ISOBEL. Tom . . .

CHERRY. Now, just a minute, dear . . .

ISOBEL. Tom, can I have my money back, please?

(TOM *stares for a moment, then steps back with a rather theatrical gesture of fatality*)

TOM. Well, I'm damned! Of all the ruddy luck. Yes, I've got it.

ISOBEL. Kindly give it back.

TOM (*nervously*) Sure. (*He takes two ten-shilling notes from his pocket and puts it on the table*) I was going to. Look, Mum. I wanted it for . . .

ISOBEL. It doesn't matter what you wanted it for; give it back.

TOM (*panting*) There it is.

ISOBEL. Tom, will you please give it back.

TOM (*puzzled and irritated*) That's it.

ISOBEL. I am asking you to return the money which you took from my purse.

TOM (*very distressed*) I have done, blast it! What's the matter with you?

ISOBEL. *All* of it.

TOM. That is all of it.

ISOBEL. It isn't.

TOM (*his voice trembling*) It is. Oh, blast it, Mother, don't let's have a blasted row. I know I shouldn't have taken the blasted money. I wanted it to take Carol out, but I didn't; I was going to give it back; I've had it on me ever since; I've given it back. I'm sorry; I know I shouldn't . . . (*At this point he bites his lip and backs above the easy chair*)

ISOBEL. You've given me one pound.

TOM. Yes . . .?

ISOBEL. You took three.

TOM (*shakily indignant*) Took . . .? I didn't.

ISOBEL. You took three.

TOM. Eh?

ISOBEL. Don't do that. (*More calmly*) Have you spent it?

TOM. Spent what? I took two ten bobs and I've given you two ten bobs—the same ones.

ISOBEL. Two pound notes have been taken from my purse; this morning, or last night.

TOM. Well, I can't help that.

CHERRY. Now, just a bit, 'Bel . . .

TOM. I don't know what she's talking about.

ISOBEL. Tom, I warn you. If you don't give them back I shall find them.

TOM. She's off her head.

CHERRY. Now, then!

TOM. Oh, to *hell* with that. One pound. That's what I took.

ISOBEL. How can I be expected to believe that? Oh, Tom— you've admitted you took one; what difference does it make? Come on, let's have the whole thing cleared up now. (*She rises and moves to the door* R) Tom, I shall look through your things.

TOM (*crossing below the table to Isobel*) You'd better not.

ISOBEL. If you've spent them, darling, tell me. I don't mind.

TOM. That's very big of you. It so happens . . .

ISOBEL. Very well, I shall look for them.

(ISOBEL *exits* R)

TOM. Mother! If you do . . . *Mother!*

(TOM *exits* R. CHERRY, *left alone, rises and rubs his hand through his hair and over his flushed and puffy face*)

CHERRY. Oh, Crikey! Oh, Lor'! (*He sits above the table and picks up his drink*) Oh, you—you . . . (*He drinks and puts down his mug*) You . . . (*He pulls a farming magazine to him, opens it and studies its pages with fuddled care, bottom to top, left to right, like a child, talking meanwhile*) That's a nice holding. (*He takes a pencil and laboriously marks something in the paper*) What's going to become of me? (*Tearfully*) O-o-o-oh, crikey! (*He drinks hastily*)

(JUDY *enters* L.
CAROL, *dawdling reluctantly, follows Judy on*)

JUDY (*crossing to the kitchen door*) Oh, come on, Carol.

CAROL (*standing* L; *petulantly*) I don't *want* to come in.

JUDY. Please, Carol.

CAROL. I don't *want* to.

JUDY (*sadly*) Don't you think you might do something because I want to?

CAROL. Not really, no.

JUDY. Oh, Carol, you are awful.

CAROL. You're always saying that.

JUDY (*admiringly*) Well, everyone says you're moody.

CAROL. Do they?

JUDY. It's all right for you, I suppose . . .

CAROL. Why? (*Fishing*) I'm no different from anyone else.

JUDY. Oh, *Carol!* I don't know how your boys put up with you.

CAROL. "Boys"? *Men.*

JUDY (*moving down stage; stung*) Boys—men, what's the difference?

CAROL (*moving down* L) Men.

JUDY. Men makes them sound old.

CAROL. They're better old.

JUDY. You are awful.

CAROL. Oh, for Pete's sake!

JUDY. Gosh, you're moody. When we have our flat we'll have to have a party every night, I can see that.

CAROL. That's what you're after, isn't it? Parties.

JUDY. Well, I like parties.

CAROL. You don't go to them.

JUDY. I do—I—I went to the end-of-term ball.

CAROL. That's not a *party.* (*She crossed to Judy*) Look: if we had a flat—and we had a party . . .

JUDY. Yes?

CAROL. And they all came . . .

JUDY. Yes?

CAROL. Well, look—you'd have to do your own smooching.

JUDY. I—I know that, Carol.

CAROL. Yes, but—I don't think you'd like it.

JUDY. I *would.* Oh, I would, Carol.

CAROL. Anyway, we're not getting the flat, are we?

JUDY. What d'you mean, Carol?

CAROL. You've been stringing me along, Judy. Johnny Odasalski's going to get that Student Award.

JUDY. Don't be silly, dear; I've practically got it. I've told you.

CAROL. Professor Herring was talking to Wilfred this morning and he said Johnny Odasalski would get it. Your work's pretty good but it's geometrical; it's cold.

JUDY (*after a pause*) Cold. (*She pauses*) Did Professor Herring say that?

CAROL. Yes, I think so. Oh, crikey, don't start yelling.

JUDY. I'm not.

CAROL. I'll come inside if you want me to.

JUDY. Yes, righto. (*She moves to the kitchen door*) You are kind, Carol. I wanted to talk to you, you see. I was going to. It'll be all right, I'm sure it will. Even if I don't get this, I'm sure . . .

(CAROL *eyes Judy, calculating the intensity of her emotion*)

CAROL (*shrugging*) O.K. Take it easy.

JUDY. Yes, all right; I will, Carol; only just come inside; it's all right. (*She holds out her hand*)

(CAROL *does not take Judy's hand but moves towards her.* JUDY, *satisfied, opens the door, sees Cherry and checks*)

CHERRY. 'Lo, dear—I—er . . . (*He pulls himself together and frowns with drunken gravity*)

JUDY (*whirling about in the doorway*) He's drunk.

CAROL (*eagerly*) Is he? (*She pushes past Judy and goes into the kitchen*)

(JUDY *follows Carol on and closes the door.* CAROL *stands above the easy chair.* CHERRY *rises*)

CHERRY (*benign, dignified and helpless*) Hello, Carol. Come in, Carol, come in and sit down. (*In his drunkenness and care he is forced to a very simple method of reassuring them of his goodwill, a garden party style of speaking, very clear, considered and slow*) How very charming you both look—it does me good to see you here. Can I persuade either, or both, of you to join me in a glass of country cider?

JUDY (*moving down* LC) No, thanks. (*Irritated*) You know I can't stand it.

CHERRY. I'm sorry, I had forgotten. (*To Carol*) Now, what are you contemplating so intently? (*He raises his hand to his head, with the innocent smile of the simple-hearted drunk*) I hope I am not still wearing my hat?

CAROL. No. Your hair's a bit rumpled.

CHERRY (*stroking his hair; absently*) That may be—that may be.

CAROL (*crossing to the table*) I'll have some cider.

CHERRY. Ah, yes. (*He collects a glass from the dresser, crosses to the barrel and fills the glass with cider*) I have had an extremely distressing day.

CAROL (*moving below the table*) Oh, what a pity. What's been the matter? (*She leans on the downstage edge of the table*)

CHERRY. I should like very much to be able to confide in you, my dear. (*He hands the glass to Carol*) But I cannot. (*He crosses to Judy. Gently*) And Judy, my dear, what kind of day have your talents brought to you?

JUDY. Father, really!

CHERRY. Is it offensive? Don't be offended.

JUDY. I'm not.

(TOM *enters* R)

TOM. Oh . . .

CAROL. Hi, Tom!

TOM (*moving to* R *of the table*) Dad . . .

(ISOBEL *enters* R *and stands, holding the door open.* CHERRY *moves up* C)

ISOBEL. Tom, what are you doing?

TOM. I'm trying to borrow your two lousy quid.

ISOBEL. And what possible purpose can that serve? Kindly come back, I'm not nearly satisfied yet.

(TOM *exits* R)

And you, too, Judy.

Judy. Me? Why?

Isobel. Because I ask you to.

Judy. Why—what's going on?

Isobel. Will you please come? I want those two pounds back.

(Isobel *exits* r)

Judy (*crossing to the door* r) Carol, don't go.

Carol. O.K.

Judy (*as she exits*) Really, Mother, I don't know what all this fuss is about.

(Judy *exits* r)

Cherry (*crossing to the door* r *and closing it*) I dislike intensely this atmosphere of tumult in a house. I am fastidious, you know.

Carol. You don't have to tell me that, Mr Cherry.

Cherry (*moving to* l *of Carol*) No, but I wish you'd tell Judy. You understand a great deal for your age. (*He holds her arm*) It's very pleasant having you here—I'm not intending to be familiar.

Carol. I don't mind.

Cherry (*nodding with a wise, sad smile*) To you I must seem as repulsively old as you are—young.

Carol. No, you don't seem old. You just seem—well—a man.

Cherry (*as one who admits a point*) One does learn *something* as one lives; there's that, I suppose.

Carol. What's this about two pounds? Has Tom lifted it?

Cherry. No. (*He crossed to the fender*) I'd rather say nothing about it, if you don't mind, Carol. Tom is deeply under your spell. We all are.

Carol (*admiringly*) Your generation is terribly smooth..

Cherry. "Smooth" doesn't sound altogether . . .

Carol. Oh, it is. Altogether. (*She sips Cherry's cider*) Phew! (*She sips again*) Gin!

Cherry (*disconcerted*) Gin?

Carol (*playfully reproachful*) Mr Cherry.

Cherry (*reassured*) You've discovered my little secret.

Carol. You must have a constitution like a bull.

Cherry (*laughing*) I'm well seasoned. (*He crosses to Carol and takes the mug*) Yes, I wish I had a shilling for every pint of this I've sunk.

Carol (*sitting on the table*) What would you do with it?

Cherry. I might buy you a nice present.

Carol. No, seriously.

Cherry. Well, why not?

Carol (*laughing*) Mrs Cherry might'nt like it.

Cherry. Oh. (*He laughs*) Well—(*he sits* l *of the table*) seriously then, if I had the money—(*he slaps the magazine*) I'd buy that.

(Carol *leans towards* Cherry. *He looks up as her face approaches, but she stops short*)

D

CAROL. What is it?

CHERRY. It's a farm.

CAROL (*twisting her head to look at the advertisement*) I can't read it. What does it say?

CHERRY. Oh. (*Embarrassed, he mumbles rapidly*) "Fifteen acres orchard and grass in ring fence with two hundred and fifty yards frontage on metalled road . . ."

CAROL. No. Slowly. What's it mean?

CHERRY. Well: "Two hundred and fifty yards frontage on metalled road"—that's very handy for getting your stuff shifted. If you've only got a narrow frontage it means everything's got to be brought in from the fields to the same gate, you see. And that means either you're up to your eyes in mud half the year or you make a paved drive, which costs money. Then "Tyings for six". That's cows, of course. I shouldn't bother with that. Cows are a great responsibility. I might just keep a little Jersey or Guernsey on just to supply the house, something like that with a high butter-fat content, bulk doesn't matter in a case like that, you'd have more than you wanted, you could have cream with every meal. But I don't know even about that. I can't stand them killing the calves. "Walled garden"—that's useful . . .

CAROL. Is this in Somerset?

CHERRY. Mendip. That's the best of Somerset. (*Suddenly moved. Gloomy*) I talk about it too much.

CAROL. You talk awfully well about it.

CHERRY. I don't know about that. 'Course, I was born there. Quite near where I think this is, but bigger, oh, a big farm, with twelve men working for us at harvest time, real men, real characters.

CAROL. That one who carried the horse?

CHERRY. That's right. (*He pauses*) He was the Lord of the Harvest, as they used to call him in those days.

(*The music of the "Flowering Cherry" theme is heard*)

Oh, harvest time was something glorious then, the horses and the men. They used to bring up huge parcels of bread from the farm; a perfect mountain of bread, and real Cheddar cheese, and cold boiled bacon under the hedge on a tablecloth; the dogs used to sit round in a circle with their tongues hanging out, the dogs the men brought, terriers and collies, they came from miles for the rats, the hares and rabbits in the corn. The dogs my father had were beautiful. From our big field you looked right over the Plain of Somerset; nothing but pasture and orchards, it's too wet for crops, it's not much above sea level; green and blue as far as you could see. (*He rises and moves up* c) The men were a rough lot and I wasn't much better than the men, but the place was something, all right. The way those old-time squires planted trees—there was an avenue of elm trees two miles long that didn't go anywhere; it's still there, I'll bet; ecclesiastical property, they won't have cut it down. That's another thing we could see up there, the old cathedral. They used to set their watches by the bells and my father said, "allow nine seconds for the distance". (*He moves below the easy chair*) It's a noble pile, that building, a gem of architecture; yes, many's the time; you could bend down and look between your legs—(*he demonstrates*) with the sweat running into your eyes—(*he straightens up*) and see this thing the Normans built, crumbling away like something soft in the sunshine we had then.

(*The music fades*)

We were as brown as—pieces of furniture.

CAROL (*speculatively*) You must have been rather smashing.

CHERRY. As a matter of fact, I was. (*He removes his coat, puts it on the back of the chair ʟ of the table, then moves up ᴄ. Reasonably*) I was big, you know. (*Carried away again*) I was feared in the village. (*Reasonably*) By the lads, that is, by the boys.

CAROL. What about the girls?

CHERRY. Believe it or not, I was a bit fancied by the girls. (*He drinks, deep-chested, and with some remnants of animal poise*)

CAROL (*eyeing Cherry*) You were strong, weren't you?

CHERRY. Had to be. Well, depends what you mean by strong. You'd have appreciated old Jesse. (*He takes the big poker from the hook*) I've seen that man take a bar of iron like this and just bend it. With his two hands.

CAROL. He must have been a bit of a dream.

CHERRY. What, to look at? Oh, my dear, incredible.

CAROL (*rising*) Can't you bend it, Mr Cherry?

CHERRY. By Jimmy! I've a good mind to try. Come on, let's drink up and . . .

CAROL (*picking up the mug*) All right. (*She moves down ʟ of the table*)

CHERRY. Hey!

(CAROL *holds the mug in her two hands with the handle facing Cherry and looks at him over the mug as she sips*)

Like it?

CAROL. Mm. (*She goes on looking and sipping*)

(CHERRY *moves to ʟ of Carol and holds the handle of the mug*)

CHERRY. Hey, steady.

(CAROL *resists. They hold the mug between them*)

Steady—steady, Carol.

CAROL (*softly*) Are you going to kiss me, Mr Cherry?

(CHERRY *wavers*)

You can if you bend that poker. (*She backs below the table*)

CHERRY. I—I can't. Well, all right. I'll have a go. (*He holds the poker at either end*) I shall keep you to it, mind.

CAROL. Of course.

CHERRY. Wait a bit. (*He laughs excitedly*) This is how Jesse used to. (*He puts the poker behind his neck*) Let's see, now. (*He brings the poker to the front*) I don't think . . . (*He places the poker against his knee and pulls at either end*) I don't think I can. (*He pulls hard and gasps*) Wait now!

CAROL. You're strong.

CHERRY. Wait! (*He begins to tremble with strain*) Wait! (*His face suffuses with colour and his whole body shakes. He ceases straining, drops the poker and stands with his head lowered, his arms wrapped about his constricted chest, his face vacant and alarmed*)

CAROL. Hard luck.

(CHERRY *gropes his way to the easy chair and sits*)

(*She crosses to Cherry*) What's the matter?

CHERRY (*his voice small*) Will you get my coat?

CAROL. Yes. (*She hands the coat to Cherry*)

CHERRY (*feebly plucking the coat round his shoulders*) Thank you.

(CAROL *helps Cherry to put the coat round his shoulders*)

CAROL. Poor Mr Cherry. (*Alarmed*) Are you all right? (*Sharply*) Mr Cherry.

JUDY (*off*) I've had enough of this. It's perfectly abominable.

ISOBEL (*off*) And you needn't think I'm going to let the matter rest there. Because I'm quite determined to get to the bottom of it.

TOM (*off*) You can pursue your squalid investigations without my assistance.

(*The sound of a door slam is heard off*)

CHERRY. Yes. (*He straightens up a little*)

CAROL. Sure?

CHERRY. Yes. (*He straightens up and blows*)

CAROL. Well, you tried, anyway. (*She kisses him lightly on the forehead*)

CHERRY. Oh. (*He turns away*) Yes; I can't do it.

CAROL. I reckon the man who could bend that could do anything.

(ISOBEL *enters* R)

ISOBEL (*looking at Cherry*) Jim! Have you had a dizzy spell?

(CAROL *moves above the table.* ISOBEL *sits on the chair below the table*)

CHERRY. No. It's all right, really.

(ISOBEL *glances at Cherry and is sufficiently reassured to let it go*)

ISOBEL. Well—I'm defeated.

CHERRY. 'Bel, I think you ought to let it drop. That's what I think.

ISOBEL. Jim, I can't.

CHERRY. For Heaven's sake, it's only two pounds, for Heaven's sake! Anyway, they'll be gone in no time, won't they? Tom's going into the Army, isn't he? Judy's going to live with Carol . . .

CAROL (*with significant blankness*) Oh.

ISOBEL. What?

CAROL (*picking up her handbag*) I'm afraid that's off. I thought you knew. We shan't be able to afford it.

ISOBEL. No, I didn't know that.

CAROL. Yes; Judy hasn't got the Student Award.

ISOBEL. She *hasn't?*

CAROL. Uh-huh.

ISOBEL. But she told me definitely.

CAROL (*preparing to go; smiling*) Yes, me, too; I can't think why. It is a pity. She's a very nice girl, Mrs Cherry. Someone's going to be crazy about her some day. It's awfully disappointing, isn't it? Well . . . (*She drifts towards the door* L)

ISOBEL. But has someone else got it?

CAROL. Mm. 'Byee. 'Bye, Mr Cherry, I hope you feel better. (*She goes out into the garden*)

ISOBEL (*rising*) Jim.

(TOM *enters the garden* L)

TOM (*to Carol*) Hey!

ISOBEL. You have had a turn.

CHERRY (*breathlessly*) Oh, no. Don't worry. It's all right, really.

TOM (*crossing to the kitchen door; smiling*) Hey. Come and say good-bye to Judy. She wants to talk to you.

CAROL (*crossing below Tom to* L) Where is she?

TOM. Waiting for you in the Coffee Bar.

CAROL (*smiling and shrugging; indifferently*) Oh, Lord! Are you coming?

TOM. I'll walk down with you. But I'm not coming in. Come on, you don't have to let yourself in for anything.

(CAROL *and* TOM *exit* L)

ISOBEL (*picking up the poker*) Jim—you've never been trying that. (*She hangs the poker on the wall*) Darling, you promised.

CHERRY. I didn't really try, don't worry.

ISOBEL. Jim, I couldn't bear it.

CHERRY. What about Judy, eh?

ISOBEL. Oh, yes. Poor Judy. But you see, Jim—she's got no money; she *might* have taken it.

CHERRY. Oh, no. I am confident that if one of them has, there would be extenuating circumstances.

ISOBEL (*crossing to Cherry and taking his hand*) Ah, Jim . . .

CHERRY (*rising*) I am confident of that.

ISOBEL. You're a much nicer person than I am—you are.

CHERRY (*moving to the door* L; *vehemently and almost weeping*) No! It's just that I'm confident there would be extenuating circumstances.

ISOBEL (*moving up* C) Shall we let it slide?

CHERRY (*not looking at her; huskily*) I think that would be best. (*He picks up his hat*)

ISOBEL. Are you going out? (*Anxious, but playful*) Darling, you've been drinking an awful lot lately, haven't you?

CHERRY. Yes, perhaps.

(TOM *enters* L *and crosses swiftly to the kitchen door.* CHERRY *opens the door to go out just as* TOM *gets to it and lounges straight in*)

(*This is the catalyst for his distress. He vibrates with irritation*) Oh, excuse me.

(ISOBEL *moves up* L)

TOM (*crossing to* C) Is the investigation still going forward?

(CHERRY *stands in the doorway*)

ISOBEL. No.

CHERRY. You were a bit handy when I opened the door, weren't you? He's been listening.

ISOBEL. Oh, Jim . . .

TOM. No, that's quite right. Some people like going through drawers, other people like listening through keyholes. (*He crosses to the door* R) It's entirely a matter of taste. (*He turns away*)

CHERRY. Now, your mother has very kindly agreed to drop the whole business.

TOM. Good. We can keep it going indefinitely that way, can't we? Well, I don't want it—(*he raises a hand in the air and gesticulates*) releasing into the atmosphere to join our other little—domestic pets up there. (*He moves to* R *of the table and looks at Isobel*) I didn't steal that money, and *Judy* didn't. Now, do you know that or don't you?

(ISOBEL *is unwilling*)

Well, do you believe it or not?

ISOBEL. Tom, I don't think you should . . .

CHERRY (*alarmed; blustering*) Perhaps *I* stole it.

TOM. Why not?

(CHERRY *steps towards Tom.* ISOBEL *moves between Cherry and Tom.* CHERRY *stops, turns and staggers out to the garden*)

Isobel. Jim! (*She moves to the door* L) Jim!

(Cherry, *without turning, waves Isobel back and exits* L)

(*She closes the door and turns to Tom*) Tom, of all the mean, vicious . . .

Tom. Why? Why vicious?

Isobel. That was unpardonable.

Tom. Why? Explain why it's worse to suspect him than me. (*He sees his letter on the table and picks it up*) Is this my call-up?

Isobel. I hope so.

(Tom *opens the letter and reads it*)

Tom. Congratulate yourself. It is.

Isobel (*a little faint*) Oh, Tom. (*She moves above the easy chair*) Is it?

Tom. Don't spoil it. I'm *half* emancipated now—keep it up a bit and you'll have a man in the house.

Isobel (*sitting* L *of the table; suddenly tired*) Oh, Tom, stop it.

Tom (*moving up* R; *also strained*) Me stop it, by God!

Isobel. Kindly moderate your language. You're not in the Army, yet.

(Tom, *comforted by the parental rebuke, relaxes and smiles*)

Tom. Okay, Mum?

Isobel (*sighing*) I suppose so, Tom. But, oh, I *wish* you hadn't taken those ten-shilling notes.

Tom (*leaning on the upstage side of the table*) Well, let me tell you about that . . .

(Isobel *opens her mouth to speak*)

No, let me, because I think this is pretty good. I was outside with Carol. And Carol wanted me to take her to the flicks. O.K.? So I said, "Wait a bit; I've got some inside," and I came back in here and—took it—out of your purse. *But*, when I went out I said I didn't seem to have any, and we went for a walk in the Park. And, believe me, walks in the Park are not Carol's cup of tea, and I had the money in my pocket—(*he taps his pocket*) all the time. And I've had it there ever since. Now, I know I should have put it back and I don't know why I didn't—yes, I do; I suppose I've just got sticky fingers; I'll have to watch it. But I would never have spent it, and I *think* I would have put it back. Now, that's not bad, is it?

Isobel (*warmly*) No, Tom, that's not bad.

Tom. I don't want to be that kind of person.

(Isobel *gives a big sigh of relief and puts her head happily between her hands like a person who has come ashore after a long swim*)

Isobel. Oh, that's good, Tom. (*She indicates Tom's letter. Quite calmly*) When have you got to go?

Tom (*looking at the letter*) The seventh. A fortnight.

Isobel. You underestimate your father, Tom. He loves you.

Tom (*after a long silence; muttering*) Some love.

Isobel (*excitedly*) He does! He was defending you just now against me. He wouldn't believe it.

Tom (*after a pause*) Yes?

Isobel. Yes. (*Severely*) You hurt him.

Tom. Now, I said, forget it. And I repeat, why was it worse to suspect . . .?

Isobel. Don't be absurd! Why should your father want two pounds?

Tom. I dunno. Buy gin. (*He pauses*) Didn't you know?

Isobel. I didn't know what it was.

Tom. It's gin. And it costs thirty-five bob a bottle.

Isobel (*rising; upset*) Do you think I'm going to stand here and discuss your father with you in terms like these? He just *gave* me two pounds out of his own pocket.

Tom. All right; but why me? Why couldn't someone have come in through that door—(*he indicates the door* L) found your purse, taken the money, and left?

Isobel (*looking from the dresser to the door* L; *delightedly*) Tom!

Tom (*moving up* L) Ah, yes, but that didn't occur to us; we'd rather keep it in the family.

Isobel (*terribly relieved*) That's what happened. Why didn't you say so?

Tom. I've only just thought of it; you're the detective round here. But as soon as a bit of money goes, you don't stop to think —it's out with the fingerprint powder, mark the notes—(*he moves up* R) that's what I find pretty hard to take, laying little traps for us for a measly bit of money. (*He moves down* R)

Isobel (*contemptuously*) The money!

Tom. Oh, yes, the money. (*He points an accusing finger*)

(Isobel *takes the notes from her pocket, tears them across and lets them drop, without looking at them*)

(*He stops short in admiration*) That was nice—that was dignified.

Isobel. It wasn't the money, Tom. (*She looks at the door* L) But I should have thought of that.

Tom (*forgiving; dismissary*) Yes. Anyway . . .

Isobel. No, I should have thought of it. There was no need to . . . Am I usually as unpleasant as this?

Tom. Mmm. (*He crosses to Isobel, kneels and pieces together the torn notes*) I'll tell you one thing—I can use these even if you can't. You can do a lot with this stuff.

Isobel (*mockingly*) Not very dignified.

Tom. Oh, well, if you can afford to chuck it about, I reckon I can afford to pick it up. (*His attention is caught by something on the notes. He cocks his head and looks again, then sits back on his heels and grins up at Isobel*) How did you mark them?

ISOBEL (*staring at Tom; after a pause*) I . . .

TOM. Was it a bloody great cross in the corner? (*He shows her the notes*)

(ISOBEL, *speechless, nods*)

(*He rises. With gusty relief*) Why, you silly woman, you *had* them. (*He sees her face and the truth falls on him*) Are those the ones he gave you?

(ISOBEL *nods.* TOM *stuffs the notes in his pocket and wipes his nose with his hand. The front door bell rings*)

Someone at the door. (*Softly*) Do you want them? (*He takes the notes from his pocket and hands them to Isobel*) Jesus! I'm sorry, Mum.

(*The front door bell rings*)

I'll get it.

(TOM *exits* R. ISOBEL *sits on the chair above the table, rests her chin on one hand and with the other she pushes the torn notes into place on the surface of the table, intensely considering, approaching a decision.*
TOM *re-enters* R *and stands in the open doorway*)

It's that chap, Bowman. D'you want to see him?

(ISOBEL *shakes her head.*
BOWMAN *enters* R)

BOWMAN. Good afternoon.

TOM. Now, just a minute . . .

ISOBEL (*rousing herself*) All right, Tom.

BOWMAN (*crossing to* R *of the table*) I've called to see Mr Cherry about the trees.

ISOBEL. My husband isn't here.

TOM. I told him that.

(BOWMAN *looks expectantly at Isobel*)

ISOBEL (*a shade impatiently*) I'm afraid *I* can't help you.

BOWMAN. May I wait?

ISOBEL. Mr Bowman, don't you *know* you're on a wild goose chase?

BOWMAN. In what way, exactly?

ISOBEL. My husband is . . . Tom, would you?

(TOM *exits* R)

(*She rises*) Mr Bowman, there is no orchard. I should have thought you might have guessed. It's a kind of hobby of my husband's. He thinks about it and makes plans about it—but it isn't a bit serious. He writes these letters to people. It's a kind of . . .

Bowman. A kind of hallucination.

Isobel (*after a pause*) Well then; if you know?

Bowman (*hurriedly*) I wanted to ask you for something.

Isobel. Me?

Bowman. I—er—(*it is on the spur of the moment*) I wondered if you'd—(*he crosses above the table to the dresser*) let me have one of your plants? (*He indicates the tray of cacti*)

Isobel. Of course. Which one?

Bowman. Er—(*at random*) this one. (*He picks up a cactus*)

Isobel (*looking down at the cactus*) Yes, certainly. (*She looks up at him, curious*) You can get those anywhere.

(Bowman *quickly replaces the cactus and stands up* L *of the table*)

Bowman (*hurriedly*) And I've brought Mr Cherry's knife back. (*He takes a small parcel from his pocket and puts it on the table*)

Isobel (*looking down at the packet*) That's very kind of you. (*She looks curiously up at him*) Couldn't you have posted it?

Bowman (*moving above the easy chair; after a pause*) I did take that round to his office—but of course he wasn't there—so I thought I'd come round here.

Isobel. What do you mean "of course he wasn't there"?

Bowman. At the office.

Isobel. Why shouldn't he be at the office?

Bowman. Well, he's left, hasn't he?

Isobel. Left?

Bowman. Left his job.

Isobel. Did they say so?

Bowman. Didn't you know?

Isobel. Did they say so?

Bowman. Yes. Some time ago I gathered.

Isobel. Some time ago?

Bowman. Look. I'm sorry if I've . . .

Isobel. No—that's all right.

Bowman. I was thinking about whether to come, you know, all the way up in the car . . .

Isobel. Did they say when?

Bowman. No, I don't think they did. I got the impression it was the beginning of the month.

Isobel. Beginning of the month! But that's impossible. That's three weeks. He's been going every day . . .

Bowman. Not to the office, Mrs Cherry.

Isobel. Then what has he been doing?

Bowman. Killing time?

Isobel (*sitting above the table and looking at the notes*) I see. Yes —I see.

Bowman (*moving to* L *of Isobel*) I shouldn't have come, should I?

Isobel. What?

Bowman. You don't even know what I'm talking about, do you?

ISOBEL. Well, I don't know.
BOWMAN No—I shouldn't.
ISOBEL. Why—did you come to see me?
BOWMAN (*nodding*) Mmm.
ISOBEL (*with a sharp laugh*) No—I don't think you should.
BOWMAN. Can I help?

(ISOBEL, *startled, looks at Bowman*)

ISOBEL (*with absolute incomprehension*) You?

(BOWMAN *grimaces a little.*
      CHERRY *enters* L *and comes into the kitchen. He is noisy, breath-less, crimson and unsteady. He carries a small medicine bottle wrapped in paper*)

CHERRY. There you are. (*He collapses on to the right arm of the easy chair and fights for breath*) Oof! Saw your car. Oof! Ran all the way from the pub. Oof! Wait a tick. (*He puts his head down and breathes noisily*) O-o-o-f. Good of you to come, old man. (*He puts the bottle in the easy chair*) Drop of this makes all the difference to a gill of scrumpy. (*He half attempts to rise, but sits again*) 'Bel, let's have two glasses. Oof! Well now, how are you, Squire? I've been thinking about what you say. (*He takes a much-handled sketch-map from his inside pocket and unfolds it*) And I think there's something in it—not everything, but something. (*A little irritably*) Come on, 'Bel, let's have a drink.

(ISOBEL *rises and moves up* R)

Now, "Beauty of Bath": all right—out. But what about "Sunset" and "Farmer's" . . .?
BOWMAN (*indicating the packet*) There's your knife. (*He crosses to the door* R) It's been back to Trapman's.
CHERRY. Oh. Well, that *is* good of you. They'll have made a job of it. Now what do I owe you? (*He pats his pocket*) Oh.
BOWMAN. 'S all right.
CHERRY. No; now—you're not going?
BOWMAN. Yes, I've got to.

(BOWMAN *exits* R)

CHERRY (*rising; surprised*) But I want to talk . . .

(BOWMAN *closes the door behind him.* CHERRY *turns from the door, his mouth making a half-framed question. He sees the marked notes on the table and puts a hand to them. There is a pause*)

(*Scared*) You found your notes, then?
ISOBEL. Yes. You gave them to me.

(CHERRY *sits abruptly* L *of the table*)

(*After a pause*) Why did you, Jim?

(CHERRY *reaches out unconsciously for his toy, symbol, comforter, the wrapped grafting knife*)

(*She cries out*) Don't look at your knife, *now*!

(CHERRY *withdraws his hand*)

(*She moves to* R *of the table*) Why did you take it, Jim?

CHERRY. I—erum—erum—wanted it. For—for . . .

ISOBEL. But why like that? Why not ask for it? It's your money —you earned it.

CHERRY (*straightening a little but avoiding her eye*) Well, I just— (*he is still out of breath*) just happened to need it.

ISOBEL. So you took it.

CHERRY (*with even a soupçon of defiance now*) Yes.

ISOBEL. And you let me think Tom had stolen it.

CHERRY. He stole the other, didn't he?

ISOBEL. He gave it back. And you sat there and let me go on and on and on . . .

CHERRY. I couldn't tell you then.

ISOBEL. Why not?

CHERRY. I don't know. You were . . . (*Desperately*) I couldn't!

ISOBEL. And never would.

CHERRY (*as one who, though humble, must insist on minimum rights*) Oh, yes, oh, yes, I would, 'Bel.

(ISOBEL *sits on the chair above the table*)

ISOBEL (*quietly coaxing*) Jim, tell me the truth about one thing. *Why* did you take it?

CHERRY. Well, I was short. (*He braces himself a little*) There's none in the bank, 'Bel.

ISOBEL (*gently*) No?

CHERRY (*bracing himself a little more*) 'Bel, I . . .

ISOBEL (*hopefully and encouraging*) Yes?

CHERRY (*failing*) We've overspent, I suppose.

ISOBEL. The *truth*, Jim. Oh, why can't you say—(*she cries out*) "I lost my job"?

(CHERRY *stares at her in silence for a few moments*)

CHERRY. You know? (*He puts one hand before his face and speaks with the tremulous, weak happiness that follows confession*) Thank God, thank God you know. (*He puts the other hand over his face and sobs*) O-o-o-o-o-oh.

(ISOBEL *rises and moves jerkily up* L, *regarding his shaking back, moved to him, but too tired to be certain*)

ISOBEL (*moving above the table; cautiously*) Jim?

CHERRY (*controlling his eagerness for reconciliation*) Yes? (*He half peeps behind his fingers. He sniffs. One hand moves out autonatically and picks up the packet*)

Isobel (*knocking Cherry's hand*) Leave your knife alone!

(*The packet clatters to the table*)

You see? You can't even weep. You're lying now. Everything you do is a lie. You're lying all the time. (*She crosses to the door* R *and leans against it*) There's absolutely *nothing* you have any respect for. Nothing! Your apples and your orchards; your dreams; your one dream—it's nothing but a lie and an excuse for lies and lies. You can't even weep. (*Her own control gives way and her face distorts sharply*)

Cherry (*rising; desperately*) I am. (*He moves down* C) Look at my tears. (*He takes a hesitant step towards her, putting a finger to his face. Injured*) Look.

Isobel (*moving to* R *of him*) You've been unhappy, haven't you?

Cherry. Oh, yes.

Isobel. And you left every morning at half past eight?

Cherry. I know. I thought I'd tell you I'd got the sack during the day, but when I got home, I liked the evenings, 'Bel, I never could.

Isobel. All right, Jim, we'll find out. (*She gets her coat from the hooks outside the door* R) We'll find out where you really stand, really. We'll find out today.

Cherry. What are you going to do, 'Bel?

Isobel (*moving up* C) We can't go on like this, Jim. We've got to find out, haven't we? (*She crosses to the door* L)

Cherry. What are you going to do?

Isobel *exits* L *as the lights* Black-Out *and the* Curtain *falls very briefly to indicate the passage of one hour.*

When the Curtain *rises, the lights come up.* Cherry *is seated above the table, fidgeting with his mug of cider, back bent, head sagging, an image of defeat, staring at the table or at nothing.* Tom *is seated in the easy chair, with his book, looking from time to time at Cherry with interest and some pity. Neither speaks and* Cherry, *becoming aware of it, grows increasingly restless.*

Cherry (*conversationally*) Do you know where your mother went, Tom?

Tom. No, Dad.

Cherry (*after a pause*) She didn't say where she was going?

Tom. Not to me.

(*There is a long pause. They go back to their initial state*)

Cherry (*brightly*) What's your book, Tom?

Tom. Coffee Spoons.

Cherry (*abashed*) Oh.

Tom (*making amends*) It's a poem by T. S. Eliot. Called *The Love Song of J. Alfred Prufrock*. It's a kind of satire, you know, on the 'Twenties. Well, on Eliot himself, in the 'Twenties, I suppose.

CHERRY. Really? That sounds interesting, Tom.

(TOM *looks at Cherry, falls silent and returns to his book*)

(*He casts round desperately*) He's very well thought of, isn't he, now, by—er—younger—or have I got it wrong? T. S. Eliot, that's the chap, isn't it?

TOM. Oh, yes; most people regard him as the best living poet.

CHERRY. Yes, I thought that was the name. (*His head sinks lower into his shoulders*)

(TOM *looks compassionately at Cherry*)

TOM (*brightly*) I bet those two girls are still sinking coffee in the *Mocaberry*.

CHERRY. Yes? Is it good, that Expresso stuff? (*Grateful, he quickly drags his chair towards Tom*)

TOM (*closing his book; stilted*) Not bad. A bit of all right, isn't she?

CHERRY (*too loudly*) Who—Carol?

TOM. Ye-e-es.

CHERRY (*too loudly*) Rather a *common* type of girl, I think. Something rather—rather *common* there.

TOM. Perhaps that's it.

CHERRY. Ah! Ah! Now, d'you know the one thing that matters in these—er—matters—*affaires du cœur*—affairs, matters of the heart, whatever it is they call them? Admiration. Shall we have a drink, Tom? (*He really waits for Tom's permission*)

TOM. Yes, let's.

(CHERRY *rises, picks up his mug, collects a glass from the dresser and crosses to the barrel*)

CHERRY. Yes, admiration, it's the one thing you need. (*He fills the mug and glass*) .

TOM. I thought you needed to be good in bed.

CHERRY. Now, I will tell you something that will surprise you; man to man, since you're going into the Army. You can't even have much fun in bed with someone, if you don't admire them. That surprises you, doesn't it?

TOM. No.

CHERRY (*crossing to Tom*) Oh, yes, it does; you thought it was all—Jean Harlow. Diana Dors. (*He hands the glass to Tom then sits above the table*) I know. Respect! Admiration! Upstairs and downstairs! Ha, ha! Drink up, old man.

TOM (*rather tickled by the invitation to equality*) All right. What's to stop me admiring Carol?

CHERRY. Oh! Well! It's as clear as it could be to me. Cheerioh, Tom—we'd better call you Tommy Atkins, now—ha, ha.

TOM. Cheerioh.

(*They drink*)

CHERRY. Mmm—how can I put it? It's like a taste for any-thing—for cheese, say . . . (*He breaks off*)

(ISOBEL *enters* L *and comes into the kitchen. She wears her coat and carries a letter*)

(*His aplomb drains out of him and he watches Isobel apprehensively. Experimentally*) Hello.

ISOBEL (*warmly*) Hello, Jim. (*She kisses his head, removes her coat and puts it on the chair* R)

CHERRY (*immediately confident*) Where on earth have you been?

ISOBEL. Down the High Street. What's like a taste for cheese?

TOM. A taste for Carol, he says.

ISOBEL (*moving to* R *of the table; smiling*) Tom, I want to talk to daddy.

(TOM *rises*)

CHERRY (*blustering*) Now, just a minute, dear, I'm talking to Tom.

ISOBEL (*gently*) Sorry.

CHERRY. He wants to get married. (*From this point the drink in him is more and more evident*)

(TOM *glances at Isobel and laughs awkwardly*)

TOM. I don't know about that . . .

CHERRY. Now don't back down. Stand your ground.

TOM. It's not a matter of . . .

CHERRY. Have some guts, man. You've no guts, Tom.

TOM. Nice of you to say so.

CHERRY. Well, have you?

(TOM *throws his book into the easy chair, puts his glass on the table and moves to the door* L. *Indignation makes his voice rise high*)

TOM. I've the guts I was born with, I suppose.

CHERRY (*mimicking Tom's inflection, loose and ugly*) Waapa waapa waapa waaaaapa!

(TOM *goes into the garden and exits* L)

My goodness, if I had my time over again with that boy . . .

ISOBEL (*moving up* R *of the table*) He was being very nice, Jim . . .

CHERRY. He was being damned insolent.

ISOBEL. He's not been rude about the money?

CHERRY. The money? D'you mean to say you told him?

ISOBEL (*gently*) He found the notes, Jim.

CHERRY. Oh, did he? That's very nice. Very nice. (*He drinks*) Very discreet, very forbearing. (*He raises his mug again*)

ISOBEL (*tentatively touching his arm*) Darling, I want to . . .

CHERRY (*rising*) Don't. (*During the following lines he circles the table anti-clockwise, then stands up* L *of the easy chair*) I may say, if you and Tom and Judy and—anyone else, if you think I'm going to eat humble pie the rest of my life because of what's happened today, you're very much mistaken. If anyone thinks because I've lost my job they can patronize and sneer and look down and *forgive* me, they'd better think again. Because I give you notice I shan't put up with it.

ISOBEL. Oh, that's *fine*, Jim. That's right.

CHERRY (*a little put off by this response*) Well, that's the way I feel. I don't want anyone's pity. That's not my way.

ISOBEL (*moving down* R *of the table*) Oh, that is fine, Jim.

CHERRY (*indicating the letter Isobel is holding*) What have you got there?

ISOBEL (*carefully*) Jim. I've been to the Estate Agent. They're going to sell the house for us. And with the money, we can buy your orchard.

CHERRY. Buy . . .? Buy . . .? (*He sits in the easy chair, a good deal sobered*)

ISOBEL (*sitting on the chair below the table*) We can get two thousand, five hundred for the house, easily—you've always said you can buy an orchard for two thousand.

CHERRY. A small one.

ISOBEL. But big enough to make a living.

CHERRY. Not much of a living.

ISOBEL. But a living.

CHERRY. But it isn't necessary, 'Bel . . .

ISOBEL. It *is*, Jim.

CHERRY. It may not be; Gilbert Grass is trying to get me an agency . . .

ISOBEL. We can do it together; I've got green fingers, you know that . . .

CHERRY. Listen! (*Explanatory*) Gilbert's got my job and he's trying to get . . .

ISOBEL. If you could find a place we could move down now. Straight away.

CHERRY (*protesting, defensive, alarmed and astonished*) But what about the agency.

(*There is a pause.* ISOBEL *rises and rethinks her approach. She begins again, without indignation, like a fact-finding commission*)

ISOBEL. Why? (*She sits* L *of the table*) Why do you want an agency?

CHERRY. For the money, of course. If there's another reason for being an insurance agent I don't know it.

ISOBEL (*again without bias either way*) But what do we want with money?

CHERRY. Oh, that's all very well, dear, when you're Tom's age. We're adults and we're not getting any younger.

ISOBEL. We've still got time. You can teach me what to do. (*She permits herself to urge him*) Why not, Jim?

CHERRY. You're not being sensible—what about the children?

ISOBEL (*rising and moving up* R; *emotion beginning to break through*) We've done all right by the children. We've done them proud.

CHERRY. They're still going to need help—it seems Judy hasn't got this job . . .

ISOBEL (*hard*) Then she can get another.

CHERRY. And is Tom to live on his grant?

ISOBEL (*hard*) It's been done before.

CHERRY. But if I can get an agency? I may not be much good in the office—in fact, I'll admit I'm damn bad in the office—but I've got a knack with the customers—no-one's ever denied that. There's good money in selling insurance.

ISOBEL. But you don't like insurance.

CHERRY (*sagely*) We can't all do just as we like, dear.

ISOBEL (*with much emotion*) But it's made us unhappy.

CHERRY (*shaking his head*) It probably goes deeper than that.

ISOBEL. Perhaps; perhaps not; why don't we try?

CHERRY. You know the old tag? "I change my skies but not my heart." People have run to the other side of the world before now; it never does any good. No, I don't think that's the answer, 'Bel. (*With conscious heroism*) I think we must stand our ground.

ISOBEL. "Stand our ground." (*Almost shouting*) For Heaven's sake, can't you be serious? (*She crosses, kneels beside Cherry and looks anxiously up into his face*) What's the matter, Jim? Can't you see how serious it is? What is it? Are you too drunk?

CHERRY. That's a nice thing to say.

ISOBEL (*nearly exhausted*) Oh, Lord, I'm tired . . .

CHERRY (*making hay, as so often before, with facile sympathy*) No wonder; I've given you a pretty filthy day. Now listen, dear; from this moment we're going to make a fresh start. I mean it; I'm absolutely determined; we're going to turn over a new leaf.

ISOBEL (*quietly, but drearily bitter*) There are no leaves left in my book. And there've been no leaves in your book for a long time. So don't sit there making promises we both know neither of us can carry out. (*She rises*) Let's cut off and root up and *go*, and do what you've always *wanted*. (*She gets a bit desperate*) Jim— look, Jim—(*she crosses above the easy chair and sits on the upstage end of the fender*) I don't know whether you remember, but from the first time I ever heard you speak, the first time I ever saw you, you were talking about Somerset.

CHERRY (*indignantly*) I remember.

ISOBEL. I thought you were a bit of a poet. I wondered then why you didn't go back; but I thought you were like a fox or something in a kennel or somewhere. And I've thought so since when you've let me down, and you've let me down so often all my bones are tender. I've always thought: "It isn't fair. He wants

E

something. Just not having it takes it out from him so much, he wants it so much." And you've known that's what I've thought, Jim, because whenever it's happened and you've let me down, you've talked about the country—so now—let's go to it, let's have it. Please.

(*There is a pause while* CHERRY *makes the mental withdrawal to yet another line of defence*)

CHERRY. Well, let me think about it. Give me time.

ISOBEL (*rising; harshly*) Time! (*She crosses above the easy chair to* R *of Cherry*) How much time? Jim, Jim, I want to know tonight.

CHERRY. Tonight? Why? Why tonight? Now, that's just wilful, Isobel. Tonight's the same as any other night.

ISOBEL. That's why I want to know tonight. I mean, every night's the same as any other night, isn't it? But some nights people get born, don't they? Some nights . . . (*She breaks off and turns to the sink*)

TOM (*off* L) Come on, Judy—come away.

JUDY (*off* L) Let me go, Tom—leave me alone.

(TOM *enters* L *and crosses to the door.*
   JUDY *follows Tom on*)

TOM. Go away, Judy—go on, go away.

JUDY. I want mummy.

TOM. I know what you want and you're not going in. (*He moves to* R *of Judy. Persuasively*) You don't need Carol, Jude—look, let's make up a foursome. You bring one of the girls from the Art School and I'll bring Sam Flemming.

JUDY. No! (*She attempts to get to the door*)

TOM (*intercepting her*) Now, I'm telling you, Judy, leave dad alone.

JUDY. He did it. He drove her away.

TOM. Now, listen—you haven't got that job and she's dropped you. It's as simple as that.

JUDY. No! It was father. You don't know what he's like to a woman.

(ISOBEL *goes to the door* L *and opens it*)

ISOBEL. Tom! Judy! What are you doing?

(CHERRY *rises and moves up* C)

JUDY (*coming into the kitchen*) Mummy! Carol's gone.

TOM (*closing the gate*) Oh, crikey!

ISOBEL. Judy—Judy, I will not have hysterics. Daddy and I are very busy.

JUDY (*moving up* R *of the easy chair*) Oh, yes—daddy's been busy . . .

(CHERRY *backs up* R)

Tom (*coming into the kitchen*) Shurrup!

Judy. She left me because of—daddy!

Tom. Hot air! Hot air!

Judy. He kissed her. Mummy, he mauled her about. (*She crosses to the door R*)

Tom (*crossing below the table; with profound disapproval and disgust*) Ah, Judy—Judy, you drive yourself.

(Judy *exits R*)

Look—Mum——

(Isobel *and* Cherry *have been immobilized and incapacitated by all this. Now* Cherry *looks up*)

—half of that was hot air.

Cherry (*choking; furiously*) Go and attend to your sister.

Tom (*firing at once*) Oh, drop dead, will you!

(Tom *exits R. There is a pause.* Cherry *and* Isobel *stand in silence, their faces expressing on the whole nothing more than exhaustion. It is the nadir of their marriage.* Isobel *clears her throat*)

Isobel. Now, let me see . . .

Cherry. Look, I hope you didn't believe that?

Isobel (*mildly*) Why not? Wasn't it true?

Cherry. Not like that. I did kiss her, yes—well, more like she kissed me, really.

Isobel. Assaulted you, did she?

Cherry (*really anxious; protestingly*) No. It was just foolery. We—I suppose—I dunno—we were larking about in here and she said if I could bend the big poker I could give her a kiss.

Isobel. And you tried. Silly chump. (*She looks towards the poker*) No-one could bend that.

Cherry (*sitting R of the table*) No, I suppose not. Jesse Bishop could.

Isobel (*flatly*) Was there ever such a person? Did he ever really exist?

Cherry. Jesse Bishop? Why, yes. He lived in this little old cottage—with the big bed and the old clock ticking. (*He says all this as though it is evidence for Jesse's reality*) He used to grow purple flowering broccoli. He could have bent it.

Isobel. Well, you can't; and if you take my advice, you won't try again.

Cherry. No, I won't, I won't. (*Sentimentally*) I could bend it for you, 'Bel.

Isobel. I'm not asking you to do the impossible. (*She sits above the table and draws one of* Cherry's *magazines towards her*) Come on, let's find an orchard.

Cherry. You do understand about Carol, don't you?

Isobel. Yes, I think so. I know I haven't had to share you with

E*

a *woman*, Jim. God knows what it is that's had the best of you.
(*She slaps the magazine*) This, I think. I hope. So now let's go to it
—while there's still just a chance.

(CHERRY *begins to understand her. He looks at the magazine, turns
a page mindlessly, then looks up at Isobel*)

CHERRY. You don't know what it'd be like. You'd hate it,
'Bel.
ISOBEL. I wouldn't. I promise.
CHERRY. We'd never make a success of it.
ISOBEL. That wouldn't matter.
CHERRY. Oh, be *reasonable*, 'Bel.

(TOM *enters* R)

TOM (*moving up* R) It's Mr Grass. It's important, he says.
CHERRY (*rising, turning and calling*) Mr Grass? Come through,
won't you? *Very* good.

(GRASS *enters* R. *He looks straight at Isobel, the underbred little
conqueror, his lips pursed over a smile of the deepest satisfaction*)

That's it.
GRASS. Good evening, Mrs Cherry.

(ISOBEL *turns her head away*)

CHERRY. *Very* good of you to drop by, Mr Grass.
GRASS. Oh, I haven't dropped by. I made a special journey.

(CHERRY *crosses to the easy chair, picks up Tom's book, puts it on
the dresser and indicates to Grass to sit in the easy chair*)

CHERRY. Well, that *is* good of you. (*He crosses to the barrel.
Deprecatingly*) I suppose I can't get you to take a glass of this stuff?
GRASS (*with an amused but disgusted smile at Cherry's cider*) Thank
you, no. (*He crosses to the easy chair*) Well, we have an agency for
you, Jim. Not mine, I'm afraid—that's gone to Hetherington—
his district will be vacant now, of course, and we've decided to
give you a crack at that. (*He sits in the easy chair*)
CHERRY (*disappointed*) Oh. (*He moves up* C) Well, that's a fair
district. It's a good district, 'Bel. (*To Grass*) Isn't it? (*He moves to
the dresser*)
GRASS. I don't know about it being good. (*With insolent solici-
tude*) Have I come at an inconvenient time, Mrs Cherry?
ISOBEL (*indifferently*) You've come. (*She rouses herself slightly*)
Are you going to take it, Jim?
CHERRY (*as though she had broached an entirely new possibility in
even raising the question*) Oh. Oh. Well now, dear, we can hardly
pass it up. (*He moves* C)
ISOBEL (*rising*) And the orchard?
CHERRY. I'm afraid that'll have to wait a bit.

ISOBEL (*in a tone of complete finality*) I see. (*She crosses to the door* R)
CHERRY. In another year or two . . .
ISOBEL (*moving to* R *of the table*) Oh, no. Oh, no, no, no, no, no.
(*She turns to the door* R)
CHERRY. 'Bel!
ISOBEL. I'm going, Jim. (*She opens the door*) I'm leaving you.

(ISOBEL *exits* R. GRASS *rises and stands up* L *of the easy chair*)

TOM (*moving to* R *of Cherry*) Go on, Dad. Chuck him out.
CHERRY. What are you talking about?
TOM. You go after mum.
CHERRY. Are you referring to Mr Grass?
TOM (*moving to the stove; aghast*) For crying out loud!
CHERRY (*his breath beginning to come short*) I've asked you a
question. (*He crosses to* R) Ridiculous! (*He crosses below the table to* L)
I must apologize, Gilbert. As you can imagine, it's been a trying
time for us all. Not that that excuses the behaviour of my son.
TOM (*moving above the table; gently*) Unless you're absolutely
starkers, you'll get after mum.
CHERRY (*beginning to shake and raising his voice*) Not, I say, that
it excuses the behaviour of my son.
GRASS (*subdued*) Is she serious?
CHERRY (*moving up* C) Good Heavens, no! I'm sorry you
should have seen this, Gilbert. My wife's rather given—rather
given . . .
TOM. Dad. Daddy, go and talk to her. Please.
CHERRY (*looking sightlessly towards Tom*) Ridiculous!
GRASS (*scared*) Well, I'll be off, Jim.
CHERRY (*smiling helplessly; his chest heaving*) No, don't go;
there's no need. (*In a tone of reassurance*) She won't go. She's too
sensitive, you know, always has been.
GRASS. I think I ought to . . .

(ISOBEL *enters* R. *She carries a suitcase which she puts on the floor
down* R)

CHERRY (*his lips trembling*) She's not going—to go.

(GRASS *sidles quickly out of the door* L *into the garden*)

(*He turns suddenly on Grass*) Little rat!

(GRASS *exits* L *exactly like one.* ISOBEL *picks up her coat*)

(*Soothingly*) Isobel . . .
ISOBEL (*moving down* R) I'm going, Jim. (*She puts on her coat*)
CHERRY (*moving down* C) What've you got in your case? (*With
infantile craftiness*) They may be things of mine. You're not going
to walk off with things of mine, Isobel; that's not fair. (*He looks
round with idiotic satisfaction at this point he has made*)
ISOBEL. Nothing of yours.

CHERRY (*paternally and implying a willingness to make any reasonable concession*) What's the matter?

ISOBEL. The matter? You, I suppose. Nothing particular. The whole of you.

CHERRY. It's that orchard, isn't it?

TOM (*moving to R of Isobel; tremulously striving to sound considered*) I don't think there's any need to go, Mother.

ISOBEL. I'm sorry, Tom. (*Comforting*) I'll write you tomorrow.

(TOM *exits abruptly* R, *closing the door behind him.* ISOBEL *turns away*)

CHERRY (*seized by a new awareness*) All right, we'll buy an orchard, 'Bel.

ISOBEL (*harshly*) No! I don't want an orchard. I want . . . (*She keeps back her tears*) And neither do you. Your dream—you don't even have that. (*She picks up her case, puts it up* R *then goes to the dresser and takes her bag from the drawer*)

CHERRY (*moving up* C; *desperation seizing him*) I'm sorry. 'Bel, I'm sorry.

ISOBEL. You don't believe I'm going now, do you? You're waiting for me to feel sorry for you.

CHERRY (*panic-stricken*) No, 'Bel.

ISOBEL. Well, I'm not going to.

CHERRY. No, 'Bel.

ISOBEL. I'm not going to.

CHERRY. N-n-n-n-now, 'Bel. What d'you want? Don't go. I'll do anything if you'll stay. (*He seizes the big poker*) I'll bend it for you. (*He smiles idiotically*)

ISOBEL. You see! (*She opens the door* L *then crosses and picks up her case*) You think I'm playing.

(CHERRY *dodges grotesquely before her and stands in the open doorway* L)

CHERRY. All right—go if you like; but watch me bend it, 'Bel. I'll do it for you. You'll stay and watch, Isobel?

ISOBEL (*crossing to the door* L; *with a gesture of contemptuous dismissal*) Let me out.

CHERRY. That's all very well—(*he moves and puts the poker on the table*) this is made of five-eighths iron rod.

(ISOBEL *goes into the garden and turns.* CHERRY *moves to the door* L)

ISOBEL (*with steady indignation*) If your dream had been a real dream . . .

CHERRY. 'Bel . . .

ISOBEL. If you'd really wanted that—*blossom*.

CHERRY. 'Bel!

ISOBEL. But—there—wasn't—even—that.

(ISOBEL *exits* L. CHERRY *stumbles down the step to the garden*)

CHERRY (*shouting*) I'll do it for you. Isobel, watch me. (*He returns to the kitchen and seizes the poker. Gabbling*) Watch me. Watch me. Wait, wait, wait. (*He puts the poker over the back of his neck and seizing it at either end, strains at it. He tugs savagely, staggers, steadies himself and tugs again, his breath very audible*) I can't! I can't! (*He puts out an abnormal effort and reels across the room, smashing into the table and overturning the chairs. He resumes his desperate tugging at the poker*) Oh, God, it's hard. Oh, God, it's hard. It's too strong for me. It's too—it's . . . (*Breathing like a bellows, he stands* C, *straddled, and the poker begins to bend*)

(*The music of the "Flowering Cherry" theme is heard. The lights fade except for a spot on Cherry and the vision lighting comes slowly up*)

(*He stumbles, grotesque and earthy, before his vision*) Isobel! I've done it! I've done it! Isobel! Isobel! Here—here—here. Oh! Oh! Oh! (*He drops the poker and his guttering breath is audible*)

(*The music softens*)

Beauty of Bath—Farmer's Fortune—Sunset—you can smell it. (*He begins to totter like a falling top and speaks with rising speed, as though it were an incantation*) And Cornish Maiden—Isobel—(*he stands a space, collecting his last breath, then, as though it were an appeal from the scaffold with the hangman's hand on the trap handle*) Beauty—Cornish Maid—Suns—Fortune . . .

CHERRY, *his breath cut off, crashes spread-eagled to the floor. The music swells.* CHERRY *turns once over on to his back and lies absolutely still with his eyes staring open while the vision fades and—*

the CURTAIN *falls*

FURNITURE AND PROPERTY LIST

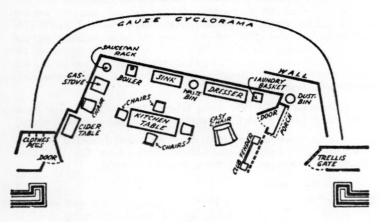

ACT I

On stage—Table (R). *On it:* check cloth, cider barrel on stand, drip bowl on
        floor
Upright chair (R)
Gas stove. *In oven:* shepherd's pie
                On stove: saucepan, kettle
                On plate rack: saucer with box of matches, frying pans,
                        oven cloth
Saucepan stand with saucepans
Boiler
Coal hod
On floor beside boiler: Isobel's shoes
Hanging on wall L of boiler: 1 small poker, 1 large poker
Sink. *On draining board:* plate rack, soap dish with soap, 4 cups,
        4 saucers, cauliflower in bowl, knife
        In sink: bowl of water
On side of sink: tea towel, hand towel
Under sink: 2 empty beer bottles
Other suitable dressing
Waste bin (L of sink)
Dresser. *On shelves:* plates, cups, etc. Tray of cacti plants, drum of
                salt, 5 table mats, 5 side plates, 5 dinner plates, 2 large
                table mats, salt and pepper pots, cutlery box with 5 small
                knives, 5 large knives, 5 forks, 5 soup spoons, 5 dessert
                spoons
        On 1st shelf: Cherry's mug, 8 glasses
        In drawers: Grafting knife, 3 small table mats, Isobel's hand-
                bag with purse and 2 £1 notes
On floor L of dresser: laundry basket. *In it:* Tom's green shirt
Table (C). *On it:* tablecloth, ashtray
4 upright chairs
Easy chair. *On it:* cushion, copy of T. S. Eliot poems

Club fender. *On it:* ashtray
On wall above door R: picture
On wall over stove: mirror
On wall up R: picture
In door backing R: clothes hooks. *On them:* Isobel's coat
At door L: doormat
Rugs on floor R and L
In garden: dustbin, flowering tulips

Off stage—Letters, bills, copies of *Farmers Weekly* and *Smallholder*, wrapped
    (ISOBEL)
    Brief-case. *In it:* file of papers (BOWMAN)
    Packet of tobacco (TOM)

Personal—CHERRY: pipe, handkerchief, wallet with 10s. note
    JUDY: handbag. *In it:* packet of cigarettes, matches
    ISOBEL: handkerchief
    TOM: packet of cigarettes, lighter
    CAROL: handbag. *In it:* lipstick

ACT II

Strike—Everything from table
    Everything from dresser top except cacti, cutlery, mugs and glasses
    Laundry basket
    Tidy sink and stove, etc.

Set—*On table:* fresh cloth, milk bottle with apple blossom, ashtray, magazines
    On dresser: Tom's book

Off stage—Bottle of gin (CHERRY)
    Letters (ISOBEL)
    Packet. *In it:* grafting knife (BOWMAN)
    Medicine bottle wrapped in paper (CHERRY)
    Letter (ISOBEL)
    Suitcase (ISOBEL)

Personal—CHERRY: watch, wallet, pencil, sketch-map
    TOM: 2 10s. notes
    CAROL: handbag

During interval:

Strike—Letters, notes, mugs, packet with knife, bottle

Set—*On table:* 2 magazines, mug of cider
    On easy chair: Tom's book

LIGHTING PLOT

Property Fittings Required—none

Interior/Exterior. A kitchen and garden. The same scene throughout
THE APPARENT SOURCE OF LIGHT IS—daylight
THE MAIN ACTING AREAS ARE—R, at a table C, up C, at a chair LC, and
in the garden L

Special lighting is required for the "Orchard Vision" effect gauze cyclorama

ACT I Late afternoon

To open: The stage in darkness

Cue 1	At rise of CURTAIN	(page 1)
	Bring in Orchard effect for 30 seconds	
Cue 2	Follow previous cue	(page 1)
	Fade Orchard effect and bring in general lighting	

ACT II Afternoon

To open: Effect of daylight

Cue 3	CHERRY: "What are you going to do?"	(page 57)
	Dim all lights to BLACK-OUT	
Cue 4	When CURTAIN *rises*	(page 57)
	Bring up lights to previous setting	
Cue 5	CHERRY: "It's too—it's . . ."	(page 67)
	Fade general lighting except for a spot on Cherry and bring up vision lighting	
Cue 6	CHERRY collapses	(page 67)
	Fade vision lighting	

EFFECTS PLOT

ACT I

Cue	1	At rise of CURTAIN *Bring in "Flowering Cherry" theme music for 30 seconds*	(page 1)
Cue	2	Follows previous cue *Fade music*	(page 1)
Cue	3	Follows previous cue *Rattle of letterbox and postman's double knock*	(page 1)
Cue	4	GRASS: ". . . orchards of yours." *Theme music*	(page 6)
Cue	5	CHERRY: ". . . better than me." *Fade music*	(page 7)
Cue	6	CHERRY: ". . . on the washstand." *Theme music*	(page 8)
Cue	7	CHERRY: ". . . farms, you know." *Fade music*	(page 8)
Cue	8	TOM: ". . . it's touched up." *Door bell*	(page 16)
Cue	9	CHERRY: ". . . of things, 'Bel." *Theme music*	(page 23)
Cue	10	CHERRY: ". . . I'm living for . . ." *Fade music*	(page 24)

ACT II

Cue	11	After rise of CURTAIN *Clock chimes four o'clock*	(page 38)
Cue	12	CHERRY smells blossom *Rattle of letterbox and postman's double knock*	(page 38)
Cue	13	CHERRY: ". . . in those days." *Theme music*	(page 46)
Cue	14	CHERRY: ". . . we had then." *Fade music*	(page 47)
Cue	15	TOM (off): ". . . my assistance." *Door slam*	(page 48)
Cue	16	TOM: ". . . he gave you." *Door bell*	(page 53)
Cue	17	TOM: ". . . I'm sorry, Mum." *Door bell*	(page 53)
Cue	18	CHERRY: "It's too—it's . . ." *Theme music*	(page 67)
Cue	19	CHERRY: "Oh! Oh! Oh!" *The music softens*	(page 67)
Cue	20	CHERRY: ". . . Suns—Fortune . . ." *The music swells*	(page 67)